THE
BIOLOGY
OF
MIND

THE
BIOLOGY
OF
MIND

W. R. Hess, M.D.

TRANSLATED BY

GERHARDT VON BONIN, M.D.

The University of Chicago Press
Chicago and London

Translated from *Psychologie in biologischer Sicht,*
published by Georg Thieme Verlag, Stuttgart, 1962

Library of Congress Catalog Card Number: 64–15807

THE UNIVERSITY OF CHICAGO PRESS, CHICAGO 60637
The University of Chicago Press, Ltd., London W.C. 1

Printed in the United States of America

TRANSLATOR'S NOTE

The task of translating Professor Hess' book was not easy. His sentences are long, sometimes rather involved, and it proved fairly laborious to put it into readable English. I am not sure whether in the end I have done justice to his very interesting and thought-provoking discussions, but I have done the best I could.

It is my pleasant duty to thank Dr. Heinrich Klüver, through whose good offices the task of translation was entrusted to me; Dr. K. Akert, for volunteering any help that I needed; my wife, Lilian von Bonin, who did much to make the manuscript readable; Mrs. Ruth Wood, who not only did the typing promptly and well but improved the text by asking many pertinent questions; and Mrs. Robin Basayne, who put my corrections of the galley proofs onto the final copy and helped with the index.

During part of the time I was engaged in the work of translation, I received support from the National Institutes of Health Grant No. NB-03180, and from United Cerebral Palsy Foundation Grant No. R-146-61. To these institutions too, I wish to extend my sincere thanks.

G. v. B.

PREFACE

On a former occasion, the author briefly discussed whether the physiology of the brain can yield experimental evidence which can shed light on psychic processes and, if so, to what extent. Today, for two reasons, he considers it important to discuss this question in greater detail. For one, in the course of investigations of circumscribed stimulations and extirpations on which we reported previously, symptoms and syndromes often were observed which were amazingly similar to spontaneous reactions generally present in certain conscious states. This led to the search for relations between stimulation and extirpation on the one side and manifestation of psychic processes on the other side. The second reason is connected with the former teaching duties of the author. The teaching physiologist has the duty to prepare beginning medical students for the various clinical disciplines by showing them the normal functions so that they may understand disturbed functions. In this connection, very little is done at present in psychiatry and in large parts of neurology with an integrated idea of functioning. Evidently, until recently the time was not ripe and the methods of experimental brain research were not commensurate with the complexities of the task. One mainly had to restrict oneself to the morphological organization of the brain; to data, that is to say, which can be gained from dead material. However, the physiologist, pharmacologist, neurologist, psychiatrist, and also the zoologist who is functionally oriented should be equally interested in the processes which go on in the living brain and which may have connections with psychic processes.

This conception was the basis for the goal of experimental investigations which, as far as we are concerned, have now been finished. We shall discuss in the first place our own observations in which circumscribed stimulations and extirpations in various parts and areas of the brain brought about primitive modes of behavior. After that, we shall discuss results which have been achieved by the same experimental technique and which are, therefore, comparable with each other and with our own results. Experiences of other authors have been used insofar as the method used by them allows (at least to some extent) meaningful comparisons.

As far as content is concerned, the author has no intention of giving a comprehensive survey. Just as he considers functional organization as the central problem of the life processes, so this order has determined the arrangement of the subsequent exposition. From a practical point of view, it was further necessary to be concise, for if I wanted to quote everything that has something to do with the subject, this could go on forever and would make it practically impossible to perceive connections. Therefore, a few concrete examples must suffice in order to discuss the ideas critically. Nonetheless, for those people whose interest in a certain question goes beyond what is included here, we have given further information in a separate list, a choice of publications arranged by subject matter without going into a critical evaluation. It should be enough if contacts with a wider field have been established. On the other hand, some experiences have been given at greater length which have become important in practice. Here we should mention the physiological foundation of psychosomatic phenomena in an analysis of the functional organization of two well-known psychotropic substances which are given as examples.

If one wants to establish a connection between objective and subjective events, one can use records of patients who had to undergo neurosurgical treatment for diagnostic and thereapeutic reasons. In a discussion of symptoms and syndromes, one can achieve communication by speech. It is much more difficult to inform oneself about the subjective experiences of animals that one observes. Although the idea is well founded that even here, sensory stimuli become conscious and that many highly organized species are moved by feelings and moods, one can with great probability base his conclusions only on indications. If one knows the "functional inventory" of each species and its "repertoire" concerning psychic effects, the various modes of behavior can be interpreted as a kind of sign language. Accordingly, in the present discussion, those arguments have been used first of all, which are based on the results of behavioral research.

For a better understanding, this work has been divided into three parts. The first is a short sketch of the psychological functions which can be achieved by man and—at a great distance—also by more highly organized animals. In the second part, we will search for connections between psychic effects and functional organization of the brain. In the third part, some principles will be abstracted which are valid in varying degrees. Also, some special experiences and viewpoints will be mentioned.

In completing this work, the author had help from various sides. In the first place, while doing this work, there were oral discussions, generally in colloquia, on brain research. Representatives of various special clinical disciplines were present, and thus a useful survey of the whole, wide field was achieved. Participants in one symposium (1950) are mentioned in special cases in footnotes. I specially have to thank my colleague in anatomy, Mr. G. Töndury, who after my retirement put at my disposal the rooms in which were housed the brain biological collection which had been built up for more than thirty years in the physiological institute. My ability to get in touch with documents and technical personnel in my former place of work was made possible by the kindness of my successor, Mr. O. M. Wyss. Valuable support was given by the grants, first from the Schweiz. Akademie der Med. Wissenschaften, then from Schweiz. Nationalfonds für wissenschaftliche Forschung and the Sandoz A. G. As far as literature and corrections are concerned, my colleagues, K. Akert, K. Bättig, and W. A. Stoll eased my work considerably.

Finally, the cordial relations with the publisher, Georg Thieme Verlag, Stuttgart, were a help in carrying through this program. The firm had formerly also helped with the publications of this author which were technically very difficult and which were published in a beautiful manner.

CONTENTS

I

MODES OF BEHAVIOR AND PSYCHIC FUNCTIONS

INTRODUCTION: CONNOTATIONS AND ORGANIZATION

If one deals with psychophysiological matter and looks around in the literature of neurology, psychiatry, and animal psychology and also tries to get in contact with works which have been developed from psychoanalytical standpoints, he will soon find that certain words are used with various connotations. This leads to the danger of misunderstanding. To avoid this as far as possible, it behooves us to make explicit the fundamentals of the way we look at those things which appear in the experimental part of this book. In general, we try to discuss correlations between modes of behavior which are psychically motivated on the one side and the functional organization of the brain on the other side; we also try to keep to an order which corresponds to the integral organization of man and of animals which have a psyche.

It is the good fortune of the author that recently well-known authors (D. O. Hebb, H. Hediger, E. von Holst, H. Klüver, O. Koehler, W. Köhler, P. Leyhausen, R. Lorenz., T. C. Schneirla, and N. Tinbergen) have successfully undertaken the investigation of behavior. Observations of free-living animals in zoological gardens and in the laboratory or of animals which, thanks to their inclination to social life, can be kept under control as family groups, are in accord with each other. It has also been of importance that there are observations and experiments in which the behavior of a subject vis-à-vis an object was investigated in learning experiments. Blazing the trail in this direction was the method of Pavlov, showing conditioned reflexes, and the learning experiments of the American behaviorists Watson and Thorndike, who published at about the same time (although the latter performed a much wider range of experiments). Furthermore, we always paid attention to the fascinating experiences with animals that had adapted to life with man so that, for them, the presence of human beings was natural. The facts, accumulated in one way or another, form the basic material from which we try to understand psychic manifestations after experimental surgery of the brain.

First of all, we have to discuss whether one can get any knowledge at all, and if so how much knowledge, concerning the contents of consciousness which motivate certain individuals under certain conditions. Here one can rely only in a very limited way on philosophical works, since everybody knows only what he himself experiences. From the biological point of view, however, one frequently gets symptoms which make one guess what goes on in another person even when one does not rely on language. To illustrate this, we quote the following case that we experienced ourselves. Together with a friend, I had undertaken a walk in the mountains. The path led over a steep incline on which the midday sun shone with full vigor. At about the top of the path we stopped, and, without saying anything, each of us went to a shadowy place, took off his pack, and went to a nearby brook to get some fresh water. Then we took some of our food and ate it. The question arises now whether this parallel behavior was really due to an accident or whether it can be taken as a proof for similar conditions of consciousness. In that sense, one motive would be to achieve relief from the feelings of heat, thirst, and hunger. In reality, there is no reason to doubt this interpretation. One cannot give positive proof, but the indications point to a probability which is close to certainty. This follows from the close similarity in functional organizations, which in its turn is founded on the detailed similarity in bodily build and on the subjectively experienced need—the need of keeping alive.

In relation to the content of the second part of this book, the use of indications has to be examined a little further. When we try to investigate experimentally the connection between psychic functions and cerebral organizations, we shall see that animal experiments play an important role. One therefore has to be clear how far one can determine psychic motivation from the behavior of men and individuals of certain animal species. To get a clear answer, one has to be very careful. As is generally known, the observer who is not especially schooled has an inclination to transfer human sensation and experiences such as moods and feelings and even intellectual functions to animals without the necessary precautions. So far as we are concerned with elementary goals, such as regulation of the body temperature or satisfying the need for water and food, a wrong conclusion is practically excluded if we assume similarity in psychic function, taking into account the particular circumstances. Indeed, it would be quite wrong to deny the feeling of thirst when a dog goes to water in hot weather and drinks. One also would be right to assume hunger as a motive if, after a long period of fasting, the dog goes greedily to his food pan. In detail, there may be certain differences in comparison with human behavior. For instance, the dog will very easily do without fruits or vegetables but will go the more readily to meat or crushed bone. Also, the dog will be more guided by his nose and less than we humans by the eye. In such a way, objective differences in the organization of the digestive apparatus and of metabolism become manifest. Added to these are differences in the sensory organs. Correspondingly, the information which comes to consciousness will be somewhat different and may determine the special behavior. It is guided by psychic motivation which is in accord with organic needs and, in the final analysis, plays analogous roles insofar as it tries to diminish the tensions which are based on vegetative functions; namely, the feelings of overheating, thirst, or hunger. In this sense, comparative psychophysiology gives, on a broad basis, views into psychic motivation where the indications are the clearer the better the observer is oriented about the functional organization of the species which he studies. The observer must be oriented to the physiological behavior which corresponds to the potential repertoire or the functional inventory.

MOTIVATIONAL DRIVES

When we consider once more the example in which we talked about the feelings of overheating, thirst, and hunger, we find now that these motivations correspond to endogenous elementary drives of behavior. In addition, memories act in the sense that they yield a finer differentiation of behavior. Exogenous influences are involved insofar as specific feelings and sensations modulate such elementary drives as hunger and thirst and also the memories which are bound up with them. In such a way, behavior which conforms to the momentary situation is made easier and the endogenous tension of the drive is alleviated. For instance, the primary impulses in the case of overheating come from increased body temperature;

4

in thirst from the concentration of salt in the blood, or from the internal milieu which depends on it in those parts of the brain which are sensitive to it; and finally, in hunger from the acute deprivations of nutrients, particularly sugar. On the other side, the sensation of coolness, the hearing of water, and the sight and aroma of food conduct my steps or my manipulations in such a way that they improve the conditions conducive to giving off heat, or that they reach the water that quenches thirst or that the sating food goes by correct manipulations into the mouth. If, by and by, thirst is quenched and hunger is sated, and if I also am a little bit cooler, another endogenous feeling comes more and more to the fore, namely, the feeling of tiredness. This makes me lie down and relax my muscles, if possible those of the whole body, and take a rest, as far as time allows it.

The physiologist knows still other endogenous motives of specific behavior, such as the sometimes severely felt hunger for air if one exerts one's self and goes beyond the ability of automatic regulation of breathing. In this case, one submits to the tension of which one has become conscious by reducing the exerted force to a bearable amount or by stopping it for a time. The positive feeling of stretching out is also endogenous. In this way, the muscle tone is brought up once more after a longer rest to a level which corresponds to the normal readiness for action.

By pointing to these connections, one comes to so-called psychosomatic medicine, which has already been discussed at greater length elsewhere (Hess, 1961a); moreover, the gradual transition from physiological to pathological conditions in the realm of psychophysiology is brought to attention because an abnormal tension in the vegetative system becomes conscious even when it is a consequence of organic insufficiency.

In what follows we will name a number of motivations which have to be put a step higher than those which are immediately grounded in the vegetativum. We should mention here first of all the drive to play, which is particularly manifest during youth. If the individual acts according to this drive, the ability of the psychomotor system to function well is increased and at the same time refined. The final result is a step-by-step increase in skill and thereby an increased probability of holding one's own. Help which should not be underrated comes from the genuine drive to imitate which gives certain goals to the psychomotor innervations and directs the harmony of movements which fulfills them by means of imitation. In connection with this is the drive to learn, which is also particularly strong during youth. This leads to reiterations and is kept up by the desire to reach the goal with greater certainty connected with greater economy of forces and time. In man, at least, is added the feeling of joyful accomplishment when something has been well done. An important factor in the development of goal-directed psychomotory is also the driving curiosity which, when we are awake, keeps the body in motion by exploring here and there. The result is a broadening of the experiences which can be used on later occasions.

To all these motivations which lead to a winning of substances or energies are added others that come from the necessity to be protected and have the tendency to maintain as much as possible the integrity of the body. The corresponding psychological motivation is experienced as a feeling of fear or anxiety. The reactions to it are movements of avoidance in the form either of fleeing or of seeking protection in a safe place (sometimes also by freezing in a certain position). According to species and individual differences, depending on the situation, avoidance of injury can also be found in threatening gestures or in open aggression.

An elementary and very powerful motivation of a special kind originates in sexuality. According to circumstances, it motivates behavior which may parallel the drive for keeping oneself alive. In special cases, it may come to a rivalry with other motivations when occasionally the sexual drive may prevail.

Many of these different drives and modes of behavior comprise partial function which may be important for the final result but which do not need to be connected with consciousness. They may be either inborn or learned automatism. When more complicated functions are involved, the results of which are far removed in time, it is very improbable that the acting subject becomes conscious of what is the end of a chain of single acts even when these are guided by visual or tactile sensations. Since the result of each step is the stimulating situation for the next step, an innate order may be assumed. In such instances, one speaks of instinctive modes of behavior as playing a useful role in securing lives and propagation in the animal kingdom. In the main, we here rely on the probably exhaustive accounts by Tinbergen (1948–52). In order to name at least one concrete example for illustrative purposes, we may remind the reader of the sometimes very artistic building of nests by many birds.

Instinctive behavior is, as we have said, tied to a certain result which is temporally far removed. Its most important character is its complete specificity for the species. In spite of this cardinal property, we have, at the present state of science, to leave it open in the case of more highly organized species whether instinctive behavior has to be learned and, moreover, needs examples to be imitated which can only be furnished when the individual grows up within his own species, and if so, to what degree.

A further characteristic of instinctive behavior is that it may be brought about by an experience in which recognition is given by the species. In our example, this is true for successful material of the nest as well as for finding the right place for the nest. Both are brought about by the sense of sight which presupposes a visual experience. The specific importance of these visual experiences is taken by the individual from his forebears.

We refer the reader to a paper by E. von Holst and von St. Paul (1960) which illustrates the various modes of behavior but is arranged according to other points of view.

SENSATION, PERCEPTION, AND RECOGNITION

When we talk in what follows of the effects of various sensory systems and of their relation to certain conditions of consciousness, we again start from primitive conditions. Of course, it is only possible with certain reservations to pass judgment on psychic phenomena which are brought about by the effect of endogenous stimulations. One can get information from a man by asking what he senses or experiences under certain conditions. With animals, of which the more highly organized species are the important ones, the first step is also to study the specific behavior of each species and then to relate it to conditions which can be objectively stated. On the basis of a long series of observations, one obtains in this way more or less clear indications of what goes on in the animal's psyche under certain conditions. A typical case is the cat that looks for a place with loose dirt and then looks around, makes a small excavation, and sits on it with elevated tail. One will not be wrong in such a case if one connects the impulse for this behavior with the sensation of defecation or micturition. Corresponding information is given by the housebroken cat when she looks for the box with the sawdust. The same applies to the dog who stands at the door, makes typical noises, and shows the desire to go out into the open. After that, we observe that he defecates. Seen in this way, his behavior is a sign language telling us why he must go into the open, and when we can observe what happens afterward, we become convinced that our interpretation was correct. There is no good reason to doubt even in those cases when an animal scratches certain parts of its body. The mechanism of scratching is automatic; however, to scratch a certain part of the skin shows that from this part a tingling sensation issues. The probability that our interpretation was correct is so large because we know of such connections from our own experiences, and man, on this primitive level, has the same bodily needs and is moved in a similar manner. Analogous is the experience of pain which is also elementary in nature, since injuries and consequent inflammation attack the integrity of the body and lead to a behavior which is favorable for healing. As far as psychic motivation is involved, it shows in the avoidance of the pain sensation with its strong negative tone which leads to keeping the painful part of the body quiet, to so-called favoring of the painful part (Hess, 1924). The negative tone of the sensation also shows up as a factor that determines behavior when a man or an animal answers to a forced movement by a rejection which sometimes is accompanied by a typical phonation. The subjective experience becomes still more clearly manifest if man and more highly organized animals try to avoid a situation that is known to them from former times to cause pain. The dog, e.g., turns around to flee if one stoops down to pick up a stone from the ground. The animal knows from memory to interpret our behavior as a signal and acts with the appropriate protective reaction.

In the realm of smelling and tasting, also, sensations of certain quality and intensity lead to characteristic behavior. This is only too well known from our own personal experiences. In fact, the sight of a fruit that we crave and the smell which comes from it both are associated with contents of consciousness which we experienced formerly, and give the psychic motivation to try to reach it. In comparative psychophysiology, it becomes particularly clear that qualities and intensities vary according to constitiution in behavior from man to man and also among different species of animals. In the latter case, the connection between the specific appetites and the functional organization of each species can generally be shown because the specific needs and the function of the various sensory systems are in accord with each other. If we know of such connections, the behavior becomes sensible and logical. A well-known example here is the sniffing advance of a hunting dog when he follows the prey, in this case quite different from the behavior of a human being who is olfactorily much less and visually much more highly endowed. Accordingly, the latter is mainly guided by his eyes.

Without ambiguity, the touch sensations are signaled by the psysiological behavior when we test the ripeness of a fruit by gently pressing it or when the cat begins to lap the milk once it has touched his lips, assuming that it does not feel sated.

One step higher than simple sensations and elementary experiences, conditions of consciousness have to be considered which have been developed integratively by a majority of different sensations, such as figures, bodily forms, or sequences of tones. A simple example is the condition of consciousness which comes about when a figure is developed out of a series of points in either a plane or a three-dimensional space.

These things are confirmed by the pleasing qualities of tones when they are arranged as a melody. Even when the various elements are experienced differentially or can be heard separately, they still create a certain order and will form a larger whole. At the same time, we are made to pay attention, which means that consciousness with an organizing tendency tries to widen and deepen the content. If similar perceptions are repeated, it becomes a peculiar subjective experience; one realizes the identity of repeated contents of consciousness at different times, which means that one remembers. Therefore, the former conditions of consciousness which become reactivated by repeating the same structure have left a trace (engram). In this way, a psychic force is labeled, which is a memory. A good example of the way memory functions is the recognition of a face which one has seen formerly, perhaps under other circumstances, and which is now automatically identified when seen again. It should be added here that animals have good memories, e.g., the dog finds his way without difficulty a second time and recognizes certain places when he sees them again. In principle, memory, which is based on sensations, is the counterpart of learning a motor skill. Both are of the same great importance for ensuring individual existence and existence of the species.

ABOUT AFFECTS

If we analyze the contents of our consciousness when we respond to olfactory or taste sensations, we find that we generally don't deal with simple sensations. As a rule, they are connected with a certain affective tone. If one analyzes fruit for its smell or its taste, this generally has either a positive or a negative feeling tone. These qualities make for a subjective evaluation that determines the result of our behavior toward this object. If the sensation is accompanied by a positive feeling tone, we go toward the object and grasp it; we have a prehensive reaction. Negative feeling tone leads to a rejection. The bitter almond is spit out. One avoids contact with feces; similarly, one avoids mechanical insults that are painful. In the one case as well as in the other, one answers with a protective reaction.

Visual, acoustic, and partly also tactile sensations, on the other hand, do not have a feeling tone. The elementary impression is neutral except when the receptors are in danger because of too intensive a stimulation and thus lead to a disagreeable sensation which one tries to avoid. Within the adequate scale of intensity, an optical or an acoustic sensation is only evaluated if it is caused by a combination of stimuli such as figures or Gestalten. If these remind us of certain parts of our experiences that are associated with olfactory, gustatory, or nociceptive sensations, then these latter motivate spontaneously the affective evaluation of the corresponding answer. The conditioned reflexes in the realm of the vegetativum (after Pavlov) are examples. Another class is individual behavior as it has been learned in previous training, either natural or goal-directed, as in the sense of automatic reactions. The one as well as the other class follows somatic needs, according to the procedure developed by Pavlov.

Apart from these, there are arguments for affective behavior that are not connected with the safeguarding of existence or of keeping the species alive. Here structure is important; it determines whether the figure can be easily understood and therefore psychologically well assimilated. If this is the case, it is pleasing. If the construction is not clear because of complex relationships or, still worse, if law and order are even contradicted, the corresponding content of consciousness has a negative feeling tone and is rejected (Hess, 1952c; Weyl, 1952; Weiss, 1955). Impressive positive examples are crystal formations, flowers, and many micro-figures which are known for their beauty, such as the radiolarii, whose visual impression does not have any physiological function. In none of these cases can we speak of advantage or disadvantage. The same holds true for the analysis, for instance, of ornamentations which have been developed in early human culture and which can be seen even today as artifacts among primitives. That experience of goal-directed training plays a role next in importance to innate disposition may be mentioned in passing in order to avoid misunderstanding. In this context, we will mention again that aesthetic effects are not attributes of the objects, but rather that in them the functional organization of our brain becomes manifest. In this sense, we have to deal with a psychophysiological basis of esthetics.

FEELINGS AND MOODS: THEIR FUNCTIONS

The effect of an impression that impinges upon one is, as we said, conditioned. It depends how at a given moment the readiness of various feeling qualities that are integrated into one's feelings are adjusted and, correspondingly, what one's mood at the moment is. The feelings that we mention here are different from the affective stimulations or from feelings which have a certain tone insofar as the latter are an immediate response to an experience. Feelings and moods, however, are psychological states which determine for a certain duration one's response to different experiences. Because they are apt to last for a certain time, there is a remarkable analogy to the tonic innervation of those groups of muscles which determine a certain bodily stance. This simile is also correct, as the bodily posture, particularly the distribution of tonic innervation in the musculature of the face, can mirror the state of feeling or mood. If after these preliminary hints one now looks for concrete examples, everyday experiences can furnish many of them. One has only to think of the days, weeks, frequently still longer periods, of sadness, hate, jealousy, elation, anxiety, etc. It is also rewarding to consult a psychiatrist's contribution because many of his patients are prey to overevaluated feelings and moods and display them clearly to the experienced observer.

Parallel to the directly visible manifestations, the excitation, when it is strong enough, spreads into some bodily organ or other whose responses document connections which also belong to the psychophysiological picture of feelings and moods. That the feelings which are anchored in the constitution can also be influenced by certain so-called psychopharmaca is theoretically important in this connection because the activation of certain agitations or feelings and moods can only be understood on the assumption that they are connected with the cerebral neural organization (Hess, 1961b).

It should also be kept in mind that animals too, at least those with more highly organized brains, are moved by feelings and moods which help to determine their behavior. Man and animals are here even nearer to each other than in the sector of the comparatively more frequently controlled intellect (Hess, 1943b). To determine correspondences in the life of feelings and moods in the sense of comparative psychophysiology is of particular interest because in this way we can learn some points about rank order and physiological importance. One also gains insight into the concrete happenings from which it can be learned how much broader and more differentiated are the moods of human beings. If one further turns one's psychophysiological interest, which is biologically motivated, to the individual's development from the small child to the adult, one will gain understanding of connections which are otherwise hardly recognizable and thereby be led to a correct evaluation of innate facilities and individual experiences, e.g., in the framework of goal-directed education.

If we now, after these general remarks, turn to the elementary components of feelings which we meet, as we hinted at, in animals, one of the most elementary feelings is perhaps that of fear. It comes into its own when an individual feels himself seriously threatened. It is at its height when the question is of life or death; in both man and animal, fear leads to an urge to get away from the danger. If there is a way out, fleeing is the innate reaction. If the situation is unavoidable, the courage to defend one self is awakened by aggression. The change of fear into the opposite feeling is remarkable, but it becomes understandable if one keeps in mind that in both cases the behavior is directed to the same final aim, namely, to be as effective as possible in danger. The choice of the proper means is a question of circumstances, which animals very frequently do not recognize (Seiferle, 1952). Very pronounced is the irradiation of fear into the vegetativum, particularly in the direction of defecation and micturition as a relief function, and, also in activation of the heart as an expression of tension which leads to action. The reciprocity between vegetativum and fear is remarkable. For instance, the latter may appear as a severe disturbance of the heart even without the individual's being aware of a threatening situation. The somatic defect comes to expression, therefore, apart from disturbances in circulation, in a specific psychological situation. For such a psychosomatic connection, one might think that a particular mental lability of civilized man is responsible. One could also think of a mechanism which, with the response of the vegetativum, again influences the emotional experience. Having to choose, the first idea has to be excluded because in animals too the vegetativum reacts very clearly to fear as well as to temper and joy (Hediger, 1961). Similar to fear in essence and in effect, but milder, is shyness; the opposite is trust or sympathy. Man is a special case, since for him better insight can lead to fear which does not appear in animals because their more limited faculties do not show them the dangerous situation.

Envy and jealousy only occur when another individual is met. Both are frequently motivations for a specific behavior. Where there are great differences between men and animals, they are in the first place due to the "art" of keeping under cover by volition the true feelings and emotions, at least to suppress their spontaneous expression; or, on the other hand, of simulating by volition.

Another primitive feeling is curiosity. By means of its strong influence on the behavior of man and animals, particularly when they are young, the amount of experience is enriched in man according to special gifts, choosing certain directions, and sometimes also narrowed. For protection, preventing a lesion of somatic integrity, the feeling of being under cover becomes important. It motivates the search for safe places, also the reliance on more experienced individuals of the same or in certain cases even of other species. Thus it may come to leading a life in a community. To keep order in this community, a feeling of rank order develops which among animals, in the well-known way, is safeguarded by force. In men, the intellectual faculties also play a role, either directly or indirectly; that is to say, via acquired or inherited power.

Added to these elementary feelings are a great number of motives which are determined by feelings or moods that are on a somewhat higher plane. If in this analysis one thinks of faithfulness, even animals—one may think of the dog—have to be included. However, in such a case, one has to be careful of anthropocentric reasoning. One has to be still more careful if one wants to talk about feelings of duty, such as that of the dog as watchdog, or of gratitude or responsibility. Such feelings are really only true for men and even then only for individuals who are ethically advanced.

On another plane, the main factor is not the usefulness for another subject, for another person, or for an ideal community. One may think of the sometimes very lively feeling and mood in the sector of the esthetic. Here it is the recognition of the productive imaginings of an order in the build-up of figures or happenings; one reacts by going toward it. If the order or laws are violated, one reacts by going away. Only man has the sometimes strongly expressed feelings of transcendental character. Because they cannot be directly expressed or evaluated, they are beyond biology. In any case, one has to be clear that the amount and width of our ability to experience are limited and thereby also is the treatment of data that at the moment and perhaps forever cannot be directly or indirectly apprehended by our senses. In biology we remain within a finite state and a finite time. Within this realm there are from species to species and from individual to individual enormous differences that become expressed in the shape of variations of character, in the widest sense of the term.

We now recapitulate the criteria of the hierarchical order of the various qualities of feeling and mood in psychology, in physiology, and also in psychiatry. Those feelings and moods are the bases which immediately subserve the maintenance of life and species. A somewhat higher plane is occupied by those moods which subserve a more differentiated mode of life by using largely former experiences. Of still higher rank are those components of feeling that lead to the development of communities when society is no longer restricted to elementary conditions of life, but becomes subservient to more embracing interests, discarding more egoistic tendencies.

MEMORY AND INTELLECT

For an orientation of the intellectual faculties, we again choose an example which is as simple as possible and therefore as clear as possible. We first fix our attention on man and base our argument on documents which are at our immediate disposal (Bächler, 1947). We think about objects that were left from the earliest human culture, those found in caves in the foothills of the Alps. These objects, the first products of Paleolithic man's intellect, came down to us because they were so well protected in the caves. At a somewhat later period, we have the artifacts of Neolithic men, who lived as lake-dwellers around the shores of our Swiss lakes. The products of intellectual achievements that were used at that time have been preserved for the critical observers of our own time. Particularly interesting in this connection are the instruments which give witness to the understanding of the relations between form and function and also orient us about the motor abilities of their users. A further advantage is the possibility

17

of comparing the inventory that goes back to different times and illustrates the cultural development instigated by the intellect.

To mention evidence which comes from the concrete tools, we first meet with the so-called coup de poing.[1] If one takes these into one's own hand, one can "feel" how the force of a blow is greatly increased compared with the blow of the unarmed fist. Whoever made this instrument had to know the connection between weight, form, and force and the ensuing results. It should not be thought, however, that the manufacture and the use goes back to a single individual. In all probability, even in the case of the simplest instrument, long experience had become concrete and thus the value of a tradition that goes back over generations is attested. Also, this was important when looking for the proper material. If even today we can find the place where the original material came from, which is sometimes fairly far away, we have a proof for the conscious idea of getting the material and also for a good ability to differentiate. The easily recognizable retouching of the instrument proves, furthermore, a certain ability to imagine things and, with that, the ability to foresee things. Perhaps, or even probably, at the very beginning, chance and primitive experiment played a decisive role. Later, however, a piece that had been selected was made to fit the grasping hand by proper retouching.

A higher step of intellectual endowment is shown in the multiplicity of goal-directed tools, as well as in the improvement of tools that had been used previously. Such progress implies the recognition of a high level of efficiency and therefore of economizing the force that has to be expended, which is synonymous with a causal understanding. An example is the axe, where the head was attached to a handle and where by

[1] I am here indebted to the kindness of Professor Vogt, Director of the Schweiz. Landesmuseum, Zürich.

sharpening the head the power was concentrated. The existence of an axe which was composed of head and shaft gives a reliable index that at this stage of development there was a certain ability of combination. Also, the finding of efficient use is proof of a conscious choice of the target of individual blows. The better forms are also an expression of the increasing improvement of the forming intellect. In this case, too, the improvements are certainly due to the collective experiences and traditions. Here, however, every single person had to collect and use his personal experiences. A certain biological scatter of the intellectual powers was a presupposition of progressive evolution. The more intelligent individuals and those more inclined to strike out in new directions were the pacemakers in improving and diversifying the tools. So far as we can judge by looking at various places of discovery, competition played a not unimportant role in the intellectual evolution; when several groups met, the one which was intellectually superior was victorious and could expand.

If we summarize the various criteria which have been mentioned as manifestations of the intellect, there is not much to be added in principle, so far as the later periods of human development are concerned. In any case, the advances were mainly achieved by each generation's building on the improved knowledge and ability of previous generations of tribes. What formerly was added slowly today by increasingly larger strides is a growing differentiation and thus a division of labor according to personal preferences and planned education. As a particularly important step forward, we should consider the increasing ability to isolate certain aspects from the total experience, to abstract, and then to combine these abstracted contents of consciousness in imagination. If both of these things are oriented toward the same goal, they lead to productive works that are based on former and present experiences.

A valid result is, however, only reached when the abstracted and combined imaginations are controlled by reality and when qualitative and quantitative agreement has been reached.

An important role in these psychophysiological functions is played by the concept that is generally called force, which makes it justifiable to explain its development in somewhat greater detail. Significantly, it is in close connection with subjective experience, as in bodily performances. This is the case when one puts into motion an inert mass by one's own force, and when this motion is kept up by overcoming friction. The feeling of a force is also evoked when one opposes the moving mass or when one tries to change its direction. As has been said of Newton, the experience of the effect of wind as a moving factor played a role in abstracting as did also the subjective feelings that are brought about by gravitation and that are objectively seen by our acceleration in a free fall. If we have gone that far, the abstraction of a moving and stabilizing force could then be connected with other experiences, concretely with the moon that goes around the earth, which is kept in its orbit by the gravitational force of the earth. The concept of force that has been widened to include gravitation has finally led us to ideas about the dynamics of the universe. In the opposite direction, this abstraction of the idea of force led us into the world of smallest dimensions, always on the basis of observations, but always subjectively grounded in the experience of our own use of force.

Of decisive importance for the development of intellectual capability, finally, is the use of symbols for certain contents of consciousness. In this way quantitative and qualitative connections can become objects. The transition from abacus to computations in the head with abstract numbers and also to computations with written numbers are concrete examples of the connection of mental work and manipulations. At the same time, we see how by the use of symbols one is in the position to master complex relations and to extend the function of the intellect into realms which go far beyond our limited ability to represent things. Here an example is the mathematical treatment and solution of physical problems, especially the astonishing successes of symbolic objectification of contents of consciousness in the shape of chemical formulas.

Another high achievement that is based on symbolic representation is the graphic illustration of, e.g., complex systems, where it is shown once more that quantitative objectifications correlate imagination and reality up to the limits of measuring errors.

Another example concerning symbols is what we experience if we listen to a piano or organ when the player, guided by proprioceptive and tactile experience, moves the keys from memory, and thus makes a sequence of combinations of tones objective. When he was a pupil he had to imitate the teacher, and guided by this higher authority, had to learn the arrangement of the notes and the motoric innervation of his hands as well as his fingers. When he became an accomplished artist, he invested playing with his own feelings by the way he hit the keys, by the rhythm, and by other means, thus giving it a certain subjective tone. If the physiologist who is concerned with the psychomotor function transfers the whole work which is given him back into the brain into a continuous complex skein of innervations, he finds himself in front of a wondrous order dynamically expressed. Presupposed is a specific, in many cases an inherited gift.

Among all symbolic representations in everyday life, articulated language is probably the most important one. By it one's own inner life becomes objective in the shape of acoustic processes and is again transposed into experiences by the listener. It can hardly be doubted that by the process of linguistic symbolization, the development of intellectual capacities was decisively speeded up. In a later phase, phonetic formulations were transformed into written symbols which could be seen and which remained for a long time. Under present conditions, civilized man has the possibility of objectifying the widest and deepest reaches of his consciousness and guiding his peers in their thinking or being directed by them. It is still a riddle how the principle of correspondence is established between the object-forming symbolism and the flowing contents of consciousness. In view of the principal importance of this problem, it is of interest to follow the development from conscious experience to acoustic objectification a little more closely. Occasion to become acquainted with this is given by observing how children learn to speak. This can be said about it: the first step to linguistic expression is achieved when the young child, in accord with his morphological development, innervates the anatomical organization which is given him as an apparatus for phonation. This happens according to a general biological principle out of an innate drive to make the Anlage functionally manifest. In a given case, the most primitive form is crying, and later a babbling which is without any sense. In both cases the muscles of expiration as well as laryngeal pharyngeal, palatal, glossal, and jaw muscles are activated. These at first unco-ordinated tones have two sequences. In the first place, tensions in the realm of the apparatus for phonation lead to proprioceptive and tactile experiences that change according to phonation. Parallel to it are auditive experiences of changing combination. Periodic repetitions take care of associative fixing of the experiences of tension as they are brought about by the nervous excitations which come from the apparatus of vocalization, and which are then co-ordinated with the speaking motor impulses as well as with the auditive experiences. In a sort of play, the vowels and consonants are gradually formulated and brought into sequence. At this stage, the drive to imitate becomes important. The child tries now to reproduce heard vowels and vowel sequences interrupted by closing sounds, by sibilants, by fricatives, and by trills. Success is certainly associated with a positive feeling tone, with joy. In the train of increasingly good results of imitation, the decisive step to use language with sense is now taken. Verbal formulations become associated with experiences as they are mediated by various sensory spheres. Seeing "red" is always associated with hearing "red" and later with pronouncing "red." In the same way, we get an association of the name of a person with the visual experience of his face, his figure, and the character of his language. During the time of learning there is thus a correlation of certain contents of consciousness with definite verbal formulations. The latter produce the former. Important for the correlation between contents of consciousness and symbols is the coincidence in the function and manifestation of innate potentials to conceptual unity. With this psychophysiological theory of language, one keeps away from the idea according to which there is something like a causal connection between objective data and correlated contents of consciousness.

If we include more highly organized animals in our discussion of the intellect, we are led to the question of how intelligent different species are. Numerous researches have been done in this direction. According to the critical findings in anthropoids (W. Köhler, 1921), we must admit in them at least a certain ability to combine things. Excluding mere imitation, a goal which is set by the desire to eat is reached indirectly by using a subsidiary instrument which was recognized as suitable. We have extensive material about less highly developed monkeys which were the subjects of a comprehensive survey (Bättig, 1962; see also p. 117). The ability of birds to distinguish, from a number of simultaneously or successively given elements, the one box in a series which is marked by the same number of points or is correlated to the number in the series, is surprising. It was shown that the animals could differentiate up to seven, in individual cases even to eight, and could abstract the number from the spatial or temporal arrangement (O. Koehler, 1960; P. Lögler, 1959). Our own experiences have been made particularly with cats, dogs, and parrots who live with the family. Also impressive were the observations on the success of training with police and avalanche dogs. Although one is surprised how well and how goal-directed intellectually gifted dogs carry out tasks which are given to them (Zunini, 1940), they must, of course, be taught in the right manner, that is to say, again, with methods which begin with goals which derive from drives, best by giving them a tidbit after proper behavior or a punishment which has a negative feeling tone immediately after wrong execution. One might ask oneself whether success of training can really be used as a criterion for a certain measure of intelligence. We are apt to assert this, at least insofar as the teachable animal shows that it remembers a connection between its behavior and the following premium or punishment. As a sign of intelligence, there is not only the ability to differentiate, but also the ability to associate contents of consciousness.

If the observations which have been referred to and others show that an animal which is highly organized has a certain amount of intelligence, the limits are still narrow and the distance from normally developed man is enormous. An example of this is the failure of the dog in the so-called detour experiment. If a fence blocks the dog's way to a tidbit that is desired and visible but leaves the way free on the side (Fischel, 1943), the success is largely dependent on chance, for the dog first walks around without any plan, which can be interpreted as a drive under the pressure of desire. In all likelihood, the results in successful training of rats are no different.

Parrots have a comparatively broad spectrum of intellectual abilities, according to the experiences of others and our own extensive ones. They have, just like mammals, highly organized central nervous systems, the ability to associate a large number of simultaneous impressions which quickly follow each other, and the ability to use these impressions, including similar previous experiences. This is documented by successful and highly complicated psychomotor requirements. There are still other signs that the parrot, as a representative of the birds, has remarkable psychic abilities. If something goes on in its environment, he shows a good ability to differentiate visually. During mealtimes he recognizes immediately if something is brought to the table which he likes particularly well. As soon as one helps oneself to it, he flies onto one's shoulder or forearm in order to get his portion by a quick grasp with his beak. He is definitely interested in toys. One finds that out if guided by his eyes he takes out of a bowl certain objects and, following the play drive, works on them with his beak while holding them in his foot (in our case always the left), which serves as his "hand." An emotional experience becomes obvious if one tries to take the object away from him. As soon as he notices the hand which gradually approaches, he runs away with the object. If one is faster than he is and gets the object in his hand, the parrot defends his "property" with energy and skill. Also clear is his active interest if somebody comes into the room and he recognizes a person whom he likes. He immediately tries to get into contact with her by flying to her or walking over to the chair in which she sits and with the same idea ascends on her leg. If the orienting gaze shows him that there is a strange person, he does not try to approach him. His behavior is very emotional when a member of the family whom he particularly dislikes approaches him. Then the bird does not hesitate to attack him with his beak. If the person, having quieted him, tries to give him something to eat, he refuses to take it if it is not a particular tidbit. Still more impressively, he shows antipathy by taking what has been offered with his beak, but then demonstratively throws it away.

Under certain conditions we have to call it intelligence if the animal is able to repeat words, even sentences or small verses which have been taught to him (for the latter see Kalischer, 1905). Obviously, he repeats the vowels and consonants in the words which have been told him in the proper sequence while they are inscribed in his memory. In reproducing them, in most cases it is probably a simple echolalia, just as in the small child during the first phase of his speaking. The parallel, however, goes one step further, if he puts certain words in the proper place at the proper time, that is to say, according to his experience in the right situation.

SYNERGISTIC CO-ORDINATION AND COMPETITION

Almost everybody knows something about this theme from his own experience. If he partakes of a particularly good-tasting food when he is hungry, he experiences a certain well-being. By allowing this well-being to be expressed in the proper way among friends, we find in this whole circle a positive mood. One finds analagous experiences if an individual is in a threatening situation. By expressing his feelings and moods, he will again transmit them to the people around him. In more complex situations, ideas which are based on anticipation as a manifestation of the intellect are involved. By using actual experiences and former facts, we understand the situation in its entirety and then undertake the appropriate action.

A particular psychophysiological constellation is present if drives, feelings, and moods on one side and intellect on the other side motivate opposite behavior. For such a competition one can also easily find examples in one's own life: the little child who has not yet been educated follows its desire for sweet things, which is rooted in the vegetativum, without hesitation. In a more advanced stage of maturation, individual experiences compete with it as inhibiting contents of consciousness. If he is still more mature, the intelligent view of more remote consequences comes into play, such as the fear of punishment if the transgressions are not tolerated. There is a competition between two opposite drives until finally it depends on the innate tendencies and experiences whether the primitive drives or the intellectual arguments win out. Generally, we will have a resolution of the tendencies in the fashion of a pendulum. Often the solution is not final. After wrong choices, there remains in the realm of feeling a residue of tension that is experienced as the voice of conscience. In many cases, particularly in people with labile moods, the competition between the various tensions of feelings, moods, and intellect becomes so strong that it goes beyond the limits of what can be borne. The psychological shocks which accompany these affects irradiate into the vegetativum and may result in somatic and sometimes even psychological errors. Anybody who wants to have a concrete picture of all this should read the biography, largely based on personal notes, of R. Diesel (1953), the inventor of the well-known and particularly advantageous engine. There one will find not only the birth of a revolutionary idea, but also the appropriate reaction of feelings and moods upon the successful use of the intellect. One learns from this historical document also the other result, namely, gradual destruction by continuous internal tensions with negative feelings. The consequences in this case were such strong psychosomatic disturbances that a long break in the inventor's work could not be avoided. Finally, he was so deeply disturbed by the pressure of the surroundings so that the reward for the work, which could not be measured in its effect, was an individual catastrophe that came with psychophysiological inevitability.[2] Another characteristic situation of competition results from the competition between egoistic tendencies on the one hand and genuine or learned roles of order within the collective life on the other hand. Typical also is the competition between all drives relating to the present, and arguments of leading life in relation to the future, be it in the same individual or between individuals of the same or a successive generation.

A field in which the competition between drives, feelings, moods, and intellect is particularly noticeable is the realm of sexuality. In this sector too, the innate characteristics of the individual are obvious. The tension of the primitive drive is opposed by inhibitions that can arise according to the situation or character either from the mood or from the intellect. The result of the competition as seen from the surrounding world shows up as an expression of conscious volition, but the behavior is actually due to the relation of inner tensions.

If we follow our program about the biological point of view, and include comparative psychophysiological data in our work, this is the place to get a little better oriented about it. One will not doubt that even in representatives of the one or the other species synergistic as well as antagonistic relations exist between drives that are vegetatively motivated and those that are due to feelings and experiences which have been worked over intellectually.

Obviously, the primitive drives generally have the first and

2 TRANSLATOR'S NOTE.—Rudolf Diesel evidently jumped overboard on a trip to Harwich, England, from Antwerp. Nobody actually saw him, but in his diary there was a little black cross after the last entry. On the tenth of October a pilot boat found the corpse of a man, and the crew took a few belongings out of his pocket and then threw the corpse, which was in an advanced state of decomposition, overboard again. After Diesel's death it was found that his financial affairs were a complete mess and that evidently there was absolutely no money left. How psychotic he really was or how depressed he was by external circumstances, it is almost impossible to say. Diesel was fifty-five years old when he died.

frequently the decisive word, but not always. Particularly when you live with others, motives appear that are in competition with genuine drives and can gain the upper hand. To go further into this would lead too far afield, all the more so since everybody who thinks about this theme can usually find concrete examples and analyze them. It should only be added that exact observations show that within a given species there are great individual differences which impress one as properties of character and of different grades of intellectual gifts.

A particular point that is related to the intellect has to do with getting used to situations or happenings which recur time and again. If the particular experience, after several repetitions, is recognized as indifferent to the subject, it soon loses all influence on the formation of the contents of consciousness. The consequence is a lessening of the psychic load which leads to a greater freedom to turn the attention to other, new experiences.

To this theme of synergistic co-ordination and competition in subjective experience, there finally belongs a phenomenon which connects the different individuals. Here we find on the one side the contaminating effect of affective behavior as well as of convincing intellectual reason and, on the other side, the so-called regression of feelings of higher order to more primitive ones, that is to say, to drives. An example of this is the reactions of an unorganized crowd.

PRINCIPLES OF INTEGRAL ORGANIZATION IN PSYCHIC AND BODILY PROCESSES

After having sketched out the psychic potentials as they are expressed by the whole organism, we now want to discuss their role in the various functional systems. The important quality of any function to belong to a certain system is its effect on the subject. In this sense, organic order has to be comprehended by its effects. According to this conception (Hess,

1924–25), it must further be said that the effect of various systems has to be related to two different planes. One of these corresponds to the regulation of the internal conditions of the organism or the various organs. In other words, we have here to do with the environment of the tissue elements and with regulatory effects which guarantee a full development of the specific functions of a system as laid down by its structure. The regulation of the internal milieu is shared by the various vegetative organs, including the neural and hormonal regulators. Thus, breathing and circulation get rid of the carbon dioxide which is formed during metabolism and bring oxygen into the "nourishing bath" which surrounds the cells. Both functions follow the varying demands as they occur during the activity of the various organs. Renal excretion gets rid of the products that contain nitrogen and thus regulates the ionic concentration. The digestive organs, together with the circulation, give the "nourishing bath" of cells their matter and energy.

Another sector takes care of the thermal conditions that are necessary for proper functioning of the cells. The exact amount of each specific effect for the actual needs of the tissue is taken care of by the vegetative nervous system.[3] The effect of its organization is the readiness of the whole organism to function. The total organism, as an individual of some kind or other, is also exposed to numerous influences from its narrower or wider surroundings. On the other hand, it creates, by actively changing this environment, the proper conditions. In this case, there are specific behaviors as regards both species and situation, which in principle are also regulators. In their entirety, they correspond to the functions of the so-called

[3] In English, the autonomic nervous system. This term is historically conditioned but it does not hit the main point because the cerebrospinal system too has autonomic potentials and the vegetative system is in reality not completely autonomic, because in a given case it might be under psychic influence.

animal systems. To them belong the extroverted sensory functions which receive signals from the space outside of the individual. The skeletal and muscular apparatus intervenes according to actual tendencies in either a prehensile or an avoiding, that is to say a protective, manner. Out of the different signals that come to the organism, the central nervous system develops images or Gestalten that activate the latent powers of the various muscles to goal-directed co-ordinated acts. In this way, the proper parts of the surroundings are made useful and disturbing influences are suppressed.

As clear as the distinction between vegetative and animal functions, measured by their effects, is the mutual connection between the two. In this respect it is of particular interest that mental events are co-ordinated with organic performances, and also that the perception of certain conditions in the surroundings leads to affects and thus becomes influential in the vegetativum. These mutual connections belong to the physiological foundations of so-called psychosomatic medicine. An example that already has been mentioned will explain these connections. If, because of strenuous bodily performances, the carbon dioxide tension increases and the oxygen tension decreases in the working muscles, then there occurs automatically a vegetative regulation according to a specific organization. If the demands can no more be met, there develops a tense situation in which a characteristic feeling comes up. The individual has difficulty in breathing, which becomes the motive to tone down the amount of bodily exertion. If, as in the case of fleeing, it becomes a matter of life and death, dictatorial impulses arise out of this distressing situation. If, on the other hand, the impulse to deploy bodily forces is only relative, a feeling of tiredness will reduce the motor activity just so far that a new, safe equilibrium is reached. If the mutual connection leads eventually to the goal, the feeling of tiredness becomes so intense that it dictates complete rest.

This is brought about automatically by getting rid of all sensory input. Parallel with this we have a relaxation of the skeletal musculature and finally also, in addition, of mental activity. Thus the whole organism gets into a state that fulfills the optimal conditions for a complete rehabilitation, which comes from rest and sleep.

From the general biological point of view, it is of scientific importance that in this change of attitude we have a regulation with a positive effect, the regaining of a tension that was lost. This is where sleep has a physiological function different from functional insufficiency or loss of consciousness from pathological causes or narcosis. The inhibition in sleep is definitely of a constructive nature as it is explained in another connection for cellular elements, that is to say, in the realm of the vegetativum.

Another instructive example of the close connection between the vegetativum and animal functions is the regulation of the body temperature, which was mentioned before. In the first place, the success depends on the ability of vegetative mechanisms which are readied for this task, either on the amount of blood that flows through the skin and on the sweat secretions or, in the case of animals which do not sweat, on their so-called panting. It is helped by the vegetative innervations of the muscles of the hair follicles whose increasing or decreasing tonus arranges the hairs or the feathers in such a way that the flow of heat is enhanced or diminished. The success of these mechanisms which depend on the vegetative nervous system also depends on the thermal conditions in the surroundings. When the external temperature is high, the success of the vegetative regulation which should lead to a decrease of body temperature is comparatively small because of the small drop in temperature. If, under such conditions, a retention of heat is unavoidable, then, as our experience shows, the individual has a definite dislike for bodily efforts.

Such an avoidance of motor activity, which is psychologically conditioned, diminishes automatically the creation of heat so that this behavior helps the vegetative regulation of the body temperature.

The connection of vegetative regulations with psychologically induced behavior is no less clear if the organism becomes too cool. We have learned that the well-known tremor of the muscles is primarily involuntary. This leads to some increase of heat production. A psychically induced behavior is added if the cooled individual finds a warm place. Then a positive feeling tone develops. Since the individual is cold, he likes warm surroundings, so that he goes voluntarily to a source of heat. Through the feeling tone, the flowing off of heat is diminished. In this way, endogenous and exogenous reactions are synergistically correlated.

What so far has been said in specific cases about mutual connections between the vegetativum and bodily behavior leads to a generally valid statement: some authors have recourse to the opposition of the dissimilatory and assimilatory processes in their efforts to understand organic laws. To this we have to say that assimilation, but not dissimilation, has the value of a physiological function. In point of fact, dissimilation is an unspecific process, merely releasing energy for this or that energetic function of a specific nature. If one always keeps in mind that organic order is in principle expressed by the success of the subject, then one phase is correctly described by readiness to develop formative forces. We talk properly about the ergotropic orientation of the organism. The opposite is the endophylactic-trophotropic orientation. This is an orientation toward avoidance of overloading the various organs and toward restitution of the tissues. Surprisingly, this differentiation of states of the internal organism is largely identical with the differentiation based on morphological criteria. We have in mind the division generally given nowadays of the vegetative nervous system according to the roots of its extra-central parts in the ortho- and parasympathetic nervous system. However, we have to note that the functionally and morphologically defined parts are not absolutely identical and that identification of morphological and functional organization leads to certain discrepancies that can be disturbing in pharmacology as well as in the clinic and may lead to misunderstanding. This can only be avoided if one always keeps functional concepts in mind when we talk about functional aspects. Morphological concepts are, on the other hand, indicated if we want to describe the peripheral structural organization of the vegetative nervous system. If one keeps to these clear lines, one also avoids the paradoxical ideas of the sympathetic or parasympathetic nervous system when one talks about central connections, particularly if these are connected with psychological manifestations. In such cases, we hit the nail on the head if one talks of ergotropic, but not of sympathetic mood, when we talk about a desire to have high motoric efficiency enforced by the hope of good success. The preponderance of the endophylactic-trophotropic system is experienced as bodily and mental tiredness with a disinclination to make any effort at all. In the sensory realm, we have a lack of active interest, sometimes even the avoidance of exteroceptive influences.

If we look back and formulate in a different way the various steps in which mental performances come to effect, the following has to be repeated: at the bottom are drives that in the last resort go back to somatic needs. They motivate drive-like behaviors for the preservation of the self or the species. To do this successfully, we also have the genuine drive to receive information through the sense organs. If this is differentiated and directed to a certain aim, an active interest is documented. In connection with the drive to make active contact with the environment and to suppress competing drives, experience also plays a decisive role, because only in that way undisturbed, co-ordinated contents of consciousness can come about. Therefore sensory exclusion, that is, the suppression of information which cannot be put into a meaningful picture, is important for the integration of experience. By combining several signals we have complex experiences from which we develop the contents of consciousness. How this comes about cannot be explained causally. The fact that we do not understand how this comes about does not change the actual relations. One must be content to understand the ability to formulate contents of consciousness as an expression of organic order whose development, like life itself, cannot be understood causally, at least not on the basis of what we know now. Only this can be said today, that information does not come to consciousness as the sum of experience, but that it is worked over as Gestalten, or goal-directed processes. With these we get signs of the positions relative to ourselves, which means the same as the so-called eccentric projection of the contents of consciousness. In their further development, spatial or temporal coincidences, allowing for a certain scatter, are motives of automatic associations to complex contents of consciousness in space and time. These are linked with other parts of the whole range of experience and are supplemented by memory.

The next step is giving them subjective value, which in the elementary case appears as a certain tone of feeling and which in complex contents of consciousness may have positive or negative affects.

Affect and memory are in close connection insofar as the former may be favorable to a so-called engram of a content of consciousness that was just experienced and also makes it easier to reactivate certain parts of the experience as ekphoria.

In the time between firm establishment and reactivation, less important parts of the experience become isolated and are lost. One forgets them. Such a loss can have negative consequences; however, we should not overlook its positive side, concentration on experiences of important parts. The same is true, as we mentioned before, for getting inured to a stimulus after frequent repetitions, when the original reactions are lost.

Opposed to the whole receptive phase, in which information is received and contents of consciousness become developed, is effector behavior. Here, motor impulses are co-ordinated according to an endogenous or exogenous goal-direction. In the resulting composition of forces, there appears a motor initiative. In those cases where the effect of a goal-direction only comes about after a long chain of various steps or where the mental gifts are small, the impulse to a target-directed action comes from instincts. These are an expression of the functional organization of the brain, inborn in their Anlage and differentiated in the course of individual development, depending on their use. If, in instinctive behavior, the end-result is not recognized, the various steps can still be governed by sensory experiences. If the organism is more highly developed, it becomes possible that temporally far-reaching motor activity will be seen and more remote goals will be consciously attempted as the manifestation of a conscious will. If a drive is fulfilled in this or that way, the drive tension is extinguished. Then the individual has again achieved the liberty to pursue other goals.

The motor expression of certain contents of consciousness has generally another secondary effect. It becomes precise just like the adaptation to repetitions. Co-ordinations which in the beginning are not very exact become gradually surer because all innervation components that do not lead to the attempted goal are stripped away. With increasing precision, we also have an economy of force and time. This whole process means learning, which is the acquisition of motor experiences that become manifest as psychomotor memory. To make this newly learned acquisition sure, we have to exercise it over and over because otherwise the action will become gradually less precise and one needs again more time and force; in other words, one gradually unlearns or forgets the complete motor action. Hand in hand with individual development and differentiation of certain motor actions, we have an increasing widening of memory through psychomotor experiences gaining in variability. At the same time, certain phases of movement become automatic. In this way, consciousness also is eased and in certain cases can turn to other interests.

Altogether, the function of consciousness becomes manifest as an agent which acts as a conscious goal-directed drive and formulates, by means of sensations and evaluation, including the use of former experinces, a pattern of impulses. Its projection into the proper somatomotor effectors activates them simultaneously or successively in such a way that step by step the movements that are projected from ideas will lead to the right goal.

II

PSYCHIC

FUNCTIONS

AND

CEREBRAL

ORGANIZATION

MOTIVATION FOR EXPERIMENTAL WORK AND METHODS

In discussing this theme, we have first to answer the question whether there are really good reasons to attempt to connect mental processes with the functional organization of the brain. In point of fact, there are quite a number of observations that seem to show such correlations. Impressive in this regard is the experience that after even a short interruption of the blood flow to the brain, for instance from pressure on the carotids, consciousness vanishes. Also well known is the loss of consciousness produced by preventing the supply of oxygen to the brain by replacing the oxygen with carbon monoxide, which prevents the breathing of tissues and thereby the liberation of energy. Well known also is the loss of consciousness as a consequence of mechanical shaking of the brain, which may also lead to the disappearance of contents of consciousness that the person had acquired before the insult, and which normally would have been ready for reactivation. This so-called retrograde amnesia is not rare and is very impressive. Psychological malfunction in malformations of the brain show that its structural and functional organization is a necessary condition for ordered contents of consciousness and their proper expression. Further argument for the close connection between consciousness and cerebral activity, that is to say with a somatic process, is given by the experience that we have substances of definite chemical structure, such as the typical narcotics, which, according to the way in which they are applied, suspend the ability to feel, to experience, or to act voluntarily. Other substances are well known which change the course of psychic processes in a typical way, such as opium, hashish, mescaline, Pervitin, and the modern psychopharmaca.

Following up these hints, it bcomes interesting to speculate whether certain contents of consciousness are correlated with certain formations in the brain. There are several ways in which this question can be answered. These correlations may depend on chance, as when pathological foci or circumscribed lesions of the brain are concomitant with definable disturbances of psychic processes. Observations during operations may give important clues. It has been mentioned, e.g., that with comparatively small lesions in the brain stem, the patient loses consciousness, while the ability to develop conscious contents with differentiated limitations remains even after the removal of certain parts of the cortex (Penfield, 1958b). A more precise confirmation is the report of a toning-down of psychic activities by a circumscribed lesion in the diencephalon (area supraoptica of the hypothalamus) which in a few minutes becomes complete loss of consciousness (White, 1940).

In a particular way, one gets clues about the correlation between somatic and functional organization by a study of twins. In a large percentage of identical twins, characteristics which can be seen are as similar as "one egg to another." In point of fact, an investigation of P. Spindler (1955) shows, apart from psychosomatic correspondences which are located in the subcortex, a genetic determination of mimetic expression. On the other hand, in movements and behavior characteristics that should be related to the cortex, there is no direct genetic co-ordination, probably because of definite plastic adjustment to the environment. In many situations, therefore, there are traits that are slightly different for the two twins according to their different experiences, and also because they like to imitate other people when they meet them.

A valuable increase in our knowledge of this subject is due to observations of animals with comparatively highly developed brains. Because we cannot doubt, after critical interpretation of systematic observations, a certain measure of mental gifts, it is proper to apply the method of comparative psychophysiology. This promises all the more success if the structural organization of the brain of various species follows in principle the same pattern. Also, the elements of the pattern, that is to say, the ganglion cells with their auxiliary organs, are in many respects the same. These facts mean that it should be possible for physiology to make important progress. What we have in mind is the investigation of well-planned experimental manipulations. There are several methods of successful experimentation, which in a welcome way are supplementary to each other. The importance of the special techniques should justify some further remarks.

The account of the experiments on which we mainly rely should start with mentioning the stimulation experiment (Hess, 1932) which was formerly used and today is very far advanced in its precision. Under certain conditions, the central application of an electric impulse or a series of impulses frequently leads to symptoms and syndromes that are amazingly similar to spontaneous behavior which is connected with mental processes. By making a record on film one is able to compare certain cases in all details, which alone gives the certainty which is needed in the extended series of experiments. After that, one tries to find the exact loci by histological control of the experimental brain from case to case and from effect to effect. If one has amassed a sufficiently large series of single experiments, one marks on an atlas of brain sections those places from which the same effect was obtained. Thus one gets an idea of the functional organization of the brain and of its systems as defined by their subjective effects, including mental manifestations.

This procedure can be supplemented with advantage by making a lesion with diathermy by the same electrode after the stimulation and registration of its effect. Thus we obtain a coagulated focus of limited extent and a destruction of localized structures. Under certain conditions, we obtain typical losses which are complementary to the effect of stimulation and which thus confirm the correlation between functional and structural organization.

A presupposition of usable results is a sufficient knowledge about the physiological behavior of the species on which one experiments. Fortunately, we have a comparatively large experience of behavior effects that can be used in this way. Another point if one wants a good co-ordination of mentally motivated behavior to areas and neuronal connections is, of course, good anatomical knowledge of the brain concerning the position of nuclei and of tracts according to their origin, their course, and their end-stations. One has to be particularly careful in those parts where elements, that is to say cells and fibers of various systems, form a dense network so that the effects of stimulation or interaction are products of mixed symptoms or are in competition with each other.

Interesting results have also been obtained by the relatively frequent operative extirpation of smaller or larger areas of the brain, where the experimenter establishes connections between the symptoms and organic defect. In interpreting such lesions, one must always keep in mind that the loss of larger areas may easily lead to disturbances of the functional equilibrium in larger parts of the brain because of the organization of the brain, which is such that many parts are connected with many other parts which are frequently far distant from them. Therefore, it is not certain that the most impressive effect must necessarily be due to the removal of an area by an operation. In stimulation and extirpation, for the reason just given, this also has to be kept in mind. Positive reasons for the functional importance of the structures that are integrated can only be expected if a very large material is available, because only then can one assume that the many potential variations of physiological behavior which one experiences can be understood correctly. As far as we can see by a study of the relevant literature, this is a sore point. In any case, one not rarely meets pretentious expressions that are based on only a very modest material and thus leave too much room for chance. The consequences are confusing; they sometimes contradict what is known of brain structure.

A critical remark on the destruction experiments should bring out a not unimportant relation. The circumscript stimulation allows a fine gradation, for beginning with the threshold its effects vary from the merest hint of a single symptom to generalized effects, sometimes with change of its character if one goes above a certain voltage. It is also important to test the connections of the substrates to a certain symptom, syndrome, or co-ordinated activity by repeating them. Added to this is the interest in after-effects when the stimulation has ceased.

Operative extirpation, however, is an irreversible procedure. According to the place and the extent of the destruction, one has frequently immediate, and in other cases delayed, compensatory effects which modify or mask the effect of destruction to a degree that cannot be determined. A very modern method works with the destructive effect of ultrasonic equipment and also with electron bombardments of microstructures. Using this technique on the cortex, a destruction of single layers has already been achieved (Rose et al. 1960). Perhaps one can achieve important progress in this way if attention is focused on the functional importance of the various layers of the cortex, which differ in their structure.

Also, the desire to recognize connections between mental functions and cerebral organization has led several investigators with success to a particular technique of investigation that has been given the neurophysiologist and the psychophysiologist by the development of electronic amplifiers. We think of leading off electric potential variations which go hand in hand with the activity of single ganglion cells and neurons, also groups of neurons, as well as of their microstructures and immediate environment. In point of fact, the possibility of demonstrating fine to very fine processes, even deep in the brain, and connections betweeen formations, layers, and organs, has led many authors to use these methods for investigation of the brain. Accordingly, when measured by the amount of investigations, these methods are at the moment in the foreground as against the classical stimulation experiments. As far as the psychophysiological use of these data is concerned, results are not proportional to it.

In any case, the correlations between the electrical behavior of cerebral structures and mental processes are still limited because the electrographic curves do not speak such an unequivocal language as the behavior induced centrally, which very often brings out normal drives. There is no doubt about the signs of increased attention if one gets out of the state of psychic indifference. The change in the electroencephalogram (EEG) becomes particularly clear in the visual part of the brain. The blocking of the basal rhythm can be seen even if we have only mental images. With other qualities of stimulation, the corresponding effect is apparently present only insofar and so long as we have an element of surprise or an emotional component. Furthermore, if we have an intention, we see a typical change in the structure of the curve. This is particularly clear in those loci where we find the cortical representatives of the muscles which are called to action. Like mental tensions, affective feelings also can be clearly seen in the EEG. The structure of the curve is, however, not a specific one for the different affects. Important is also the objectification of the readiness for action or reaction which can be seen in the EEG. This becomes particularly clear in comparing curves which have been obtained during wakefulness and sleep. However, the type of sleep curve is not always unequivocal. It can also be observed in other states which are connected with the diminution of consciousness, about which we will talk later. We have, so far, only a limited number of observations about definite electroencephalographic expressions of certain contents of consciousness. Certain correspondences between the records from single cortical cells and subjective experiences, such as visual contrast phenomena, are an important result of the EEG analysis of cerebral processes. Just as, after dark, light becomes accentuated, so the electrical activity in the cells of the visual sphere is accentuated by going from dark to light. Through these experiences and through parallel findings of after-images and nervous impulses, a correlation between the subjective experiences and an objective registration is seen by the observer. We will talk about other analogous findings later (Jung, 1961).

Another particular experience is the fact that optic stimulation of the retina leads to neuronal reactions in which a number of elements of the visual sphere of the cortex are activated, while other elements become inhibited. This behavior prevents a shift of the average level of excitation within circumscribed parts which stabilizes the ability to respond to incoming impulses (Jung, 1954). As subjective correlation, we have to assume an insurance of proportional sensitivity of the visual apparatus, even if used for a long time.

Finally, we have to consider the analysis of the effect of biologically active substances such as strychnine or eserine (which suppresses the catabolism of acetylcholine). Even with the smallest doses given on the surface of the cortex or by injection into certain parts of the cerebral reticular system, definite changes in the expression of consciousness appear (Hess, 1924, 1925). One also gets important results if, under certain conditions, minimal amounts of other substances are brought into the ventricles themselves (Feldberg and Sherwood, 1954). Not last, we have to think of the heuristic use of certain psychopharmaca which are taken by mouth, and get to the brain by way of the blood after absorption in the intestinal tract; these evidently exert a specific influence on the properties of certain neuronal structures and also become manifest mentally. The better one knows the principles which are at the bottom of the formal organization of the brain, the better insight into the psychic processes is gained by interpreting them.

It should also be said that a knowledge of the laws that become manifest by a critically oriented psychoanalysis can be useful to clear up the questions in which we are interested.

In all probability, the use of psychopharmaca in mental disease gives some clues according to the principle "ex juvantibus" about the intimate workings of the mind just as about the demonstration of connections between disturbances of the hormonal system and anomalies in mental life (Bleuler, 1953). If we include such clinical cases in the analysis of the connection between cerebral organization and mental functions, a deeper knowledge of the organizing principles cannot be missed without disadvantage. A particularly promising experimental setup rests on the combination of training for certain behavior with experimental lesions. The learning of complex acts is regarded as an expression of mental ability, particularly as documentation of the effect of memory. Furthermore, one has the impression that experimental animals of certain species have a certain understanding for the learned task. One may think, e.g., of the police dog who after being made to smell an object, uses the smell to follow the spoor, to search for the culprit, and to point him out. The avalanche dog, too, evidently knows what is involved when he is used. Understanding of the expected task has also been credited to the laboring elephant who reacts to signs, carefully lifts logs with his trunk, and under guidance transports them to a certain place. That monkeys, too, can be trained for certain goals is well known. Animals with relatively highly organized brains recognize situations in which the learned behavior is inadequate. Unforeseen hurdles, which were not used in the training, may be spontaneously and properly taken care of. If an animal suitable for the combined experiment has been sufficiently trained so that it works without errors, that is to say, reacts on a certain signal with a learned behavior, the experimenter then goes over to the second act of his research, in which a certain circumscribed part of the brain is taken out (Konorski, 1948, 1961). If it is seen afterwards that the trained acts are no longer, or only under certain conditions imperfectly, executed, then this defect becomes an argument that that part of the brain is somehow used in the learning function. On the probability with which this assumption can be considered unequivocal, we shall have to say some more when we report on concrete results.

As an important means of acquiring knowledge, we finally have to mention the morphological study of the brain and fibers and their nuclei as regards their position and connections. Added to these are criteria concerning the dimensions, the shapes, and intracellular structures. That in spite of highly developed training techniques, much is still hidden of func-tional importance cannot be doubted and has to be taken into account when we interpret psychophysiological findings. This is particularly true of characteristic properties of nervous substances which play their proper role in the processes of excitation and which are bound to submicroscopic carriers. This makes it also understandable that even the most complete examination of the dead brain can never lead to a complete understanding of its functional organization.

READINESS TO ACT

After these methodological preliminaries we now come to the more detailed description of concrete findings. As in part I, we will again consider the effect of drives which are meant to extinguish tensions and which originate in vegetative needs. The presupposition is a waking state and contact with the sur-roundings, so that usable things may be grasped and harmful things may be avoided or opposed; that is to say, so that both so-called prehensive and protective behavior are possible. To these belong observations and experiments in which, by thermocoagulation, bilateral symmetrical foci were placed with fine electrodes in the region of the diencephalon and adjacent parts of the brains of cats. If these foci are not too small, a typical picture arises, corresponding to a far-reaching loss of initiative. With somewhat larger foci, spontaneity is re-duced to a minimum. The animal lies on its bed. By means of external stimuli, reactions can be elicited, for instance, a look-ing up, but the threshold is much higher than normal. If stimulation goes on for some time, and when necessary is made even stronger, the cat will arise and change its position. If milk is poured into its mouth, it is reluctantly taken, but only if the milk is in direct contact with the lips. In such a case, some milk is taken by licking. These licking movements will shortly cease, even if the stimulus is prolonged, and the head, which was somewhat raised while the milk was licked up, sinks down again on the floor (Hess, 1954a).

This lack of initiative is further shown in the fact that the care of the skin, that is, the innate drive to keep the pelt clean by systematic licking, is neglected. Thus the pelt very soon becomes ragged and remains wet and dirty. This is particularly due to the fact that the cat no longer assumes the normal position for defecation and micturition. Lack of initiative, called adynamia, is shown in still other ways. If the cat which has lesions in the hypothalamus is brought into an unnatural position, it will assume a normal position only gradually or not at all. Otherwise, there is a strong inclination to remain in any position (Stoll, 1943; Hess, 1954a).

Apart from this lack of impulses in the motor and sensory sectors, various symptoms in the realm of the vegetativum can be mentioned. This is of interest because it points to a part of the brain which makes its influence felt in animal as well as vegetative functions. These observations are, therefore, an experimental contribution to "psychosomatic medicine." About particular effects, the following results have been noted: the temperature of the body is below normal and the metabolism, as measured by the formation of carbon dioxide and by the uptake of oxygen, is definitely diminished. Also, the diminution in intake of nourishment is clear, which means the same as lack of hunger. This shows how in the hypothalamus extroverted activity, including mental behavior, is connected with the regulation of the internal milieu. Both together correspond to a lack of readiness for action or reaction.

As far as localization of foci is concerned, it depends on whether they are more in the caudal or the rostral end of the hypothalamus. In the first case, the functional defects are particularly pronounced in the ergotropic sector from which, as mentioned elsewhere, the energetic actions are controlled (p. 33). In the latter case, insufficiencies in the realm of the endophylactic-trophotropic functions are predominant (p. 33). In summary, this shows a leading influence of the hypothalamus on the readiness of the most diverse functional systems, including the mental ones.

Furthermore, we have learned about a phenomenon that expresses a deep change of the functional readiness and is due to a specific connection with circumscribed parts of the brain. In these experiments, we deal again with the effect of central electric stimulation. Under definite conditions, the sensory thresholds are much higher, particularly clearly of the auditive and the visual system, but also of the tactile and proprioceptive system (Hess, 1929, 1944, 1954a and b, 1961c). In consequence, there is a diminution of sensory input to the central nervous system, which is thus kept quiet. As far as original stimuli are concerned, a correlated mechanism can be demonstrated even in the peripheral organ of reception, among others in the eye, where the pupils become much narrower and thus shade the photoreceptors in the retina. The damping of hearing becomes obvious if one makes a noise to which the cat normally reacts with increased and directed attention. The change in the thresholds of touch and proprioception is shown if one touches the cat and lifts it up. She may open her eyes and keep upright for a while when she is put on her feet but finally, after closing her eyes, she will lie down again. With this change of stimulus-connected readiness for sensory functions, there is a change in the somatomotor innervation. The tonus of the muscles seems to sink to a minimum. Obviously tired, the animal looks for a resting place, lies down, and coils up or, apparently depending on the temperature of the room, lies flat on one side as under normal conditions the sleeping cat will do (Grimm, 1956).

When one makes experiments in chickens, one finds behavior which has been described as a drive to sleep and which confirms our own observations. Important is the proof of the active character of the sleep function and of its connection with the brain stem.

From one's own experience one knows that in deep sleep consciousness is more or less completely suspended, except for a limited readiness to function of the sensory organs and of the psychomotor apparatus.

How the psychic processes are affected can in our own experiments occasionally be shown in dogs; namely, when these move the anterior extremities as for locomotion and give out a phonation characteristic of anxiety. One is better oriented by experiences in man because the sleep is frequently disturbed by dreams. Because the contents of consciousness are not controlled by the sensory organization, they go their own unreal way which is determined by episodes from memory and by feelings and moods which are endogenously motivated. An exogenous component may be involved and a selective attention may be taken over from wakefulness into sleep. The best-known example of that is the mother who when asleep reacts in a proper way to signs of unrest of her baby, but not to sometimes much stronger acoustic stimuli from elsewhere. Analogously, one observes in the experiment, apart from extraordinary cases, frequently a damping effect of central stimulation that is not complete. The cat may remain, for instance, with lowered head, in a sitting position but react to a disturbance from outside only when it is really massive. In other cases, she lies down in a sleeping position, although her susceptibility to sensory stimuli is less diminished as far as her readiness to function is concerned. Thus one can see cases in which the accent of the suppression set by the stimulus can be either in the somatomotor or in the sensory sphere. It thus shows us that the readiness for action and reaction of consciousness can be influenced gradually and for different contents, because the ability to activate and formulate contents of consciousness is relative.

This is also shown in motor activity from suppression in somnambulists; the higher sensory functions do not work but the co-ordinated motor ability with the closely correlated organs of equilibrium, including proprioceptive organs, is functioning. The adaptation to external circumstances is also proved by the horse who is in a strange stable close to a neighbor whom he does not know; he does not lie down as usual, but sleeps standing up. The muscles that are used for standing therefore remain in tonus under the influence of special conditions. In the sensory realm, one finds especial attention in the watchdog during sleep. He is not in the least disturbed by usual noises, but he is disturbed, for instance, by light steps which are strange to him. All these symptoms definitely delimit the regulated suppression of readiness from the uncontrolled loss of the faculties that are available in wakefulness, such as happens in fainting, in narcosis, or in coma.

After these findings there remains the question of a substrate or substrates that bring about the normal rest in sleep. This is found out by the specific location of the electrodes by which one can induce experimentally the suspension of readiness to function. The important positions for stimulation are found in a generally rather large paramedian field on the side of the massa intermedia. This so-called somnogenous zone in the diencephalon, which in front goes as far as the anterior nucleus of the thalamus, is made wider, as modern findings show, by other substrates with similar effect (Akert, Koella, and Hess, 1952; Parmeggiani, 1960; Akert and Andersson, 1951; Lilly, 1958; Moruzzi, Rossi, and Zanchetti, 1958; Batini et al., 1959). Further experiments will probably allow a more precise localization.

As an objective criterion of increased attention, that is to say increased sensory readiness, a certain type of curve has to be considered which one obtains by leading off electric potentials from the cortex. Remarkable is the possibility of getting similar curves on stimulation in the region of the reticular formation (Moruzzi and Magoun, 1949; Moruzzi, 1958), which therefore is called the "activating system." Insofar as its function is brought in connection with awakening out of sleep and thus with a unification of consciousness, further clarification is necessary, because there is a definite difference in the temporal sequences of normal psychological awakening on the one side and of much quicker electroencephalographic manifestation of activity as a consequence of stimulation of the reticular formation on the other side.

Quite recently, other interesting electrographic experiments have been brought together in a symposium on the nature of sleep. At the moment, there is only a short abstract of papers available (Ciba Foundation, 1961). Results which have become known to us in greater detail will be reported on later (p. 103). Apart from this, the findings which have been reported are methodologically definitely one-sided, particularly insofar as the correlations between neuronal processes and contents of consciousness are concerned.

A very unique change of the functional readiness is observed in the state of hypnosis. A physiologist has to consider that a narrowing of consciousness may be involved, as normally occurs when the attention is focused on a certain thing or process. The observation first made by Pavlov, that in some dogs the failure to feed that would normally occur after a conditioning stimulus leads to a sleep-like state, is interpreted by the experimenter as a spreading of the suppression of the trained reaction. Perhaps, however, this may be primarily a hypnosis in consequence of a narrowly focused expectation. As a second effect, the changeover into sleep is perfectly possible. Apart from this, this theme has to be left to the psychiatrist, the neurologist, and those psychophysiologists who have a large practical experience with hypnosis.

RELATIONS BETWEEN DRIVES AND CEREBRAL ORGANIZATION

The affective defense is among the most noticeable instinctual behavior which occurs in response to electrical stimulation. We have made detailed studies of this behavior in records (Hess and Brügger, 1943a; Hess, 1954a; Hess, 1956). A short survey, therefore, will be sufficient here. We shall especially treat the question whether it is only unconsciousness playing off a neural disposition or whether it is the manifestation of an instinctual content of consciousness. The stimulation experiments give the following data: A few seconds after the beginning of stimulation, the cat begins to spit and hiss. The hairs of the tail become erect, as do those of the back; the pupils enlarge; the whole complex corresponds to the well-known threatening behavior, as, for instance, when the cat finds itself opposite an enemy, e.g., a dog who wants to attack it. Generally, in the experiments one does not see the hunching of the back. More frequently, the animal lowers itself; this variation of natural behavior is supposed to correspond to the behavior against an inimical fellow of its own species who is not considered to be too dangerous.

If one or the other form of this classic protective reaction is completely expressed, the animal receiving a central stimulus keeps his eyes on the person close to her. If this person holds his hand out and the cat is somewhat more strongly stimulated, it attacks with its paw, its claws extended. If the stimulation is continued, and perhaps even made still stronger, the cat gets ready to jump at the enemy, that is to say, at the nearest collaborator of the team. This can hardly be understood, unless a reactive attacking mood is brought about by the central stimulation and, corresponding to the momentary environment, this leads to a reaction which is appropriate to the mental situation. If one immediately stops the stimulation, the attack can be avoided and the animal soon becomes quiet. In the activation of all effectors that are co-ordinated in the threatening gesture and the defense by attack, a direct stimulation of the motor points that give rise to this behavior is not possible, because from very different places in the relatively large area that gives rise to this function, corresponding behaviors can be induced; that is to say, behaviors that figure in the repertoire of the cat as an expression of feeling to be seriously threatened. In this way, the contents of consciousness are mobilized and co-ordinated. That the cat is psychologically stimulated by electric currents is indicated by the fact that in some cases the experimental animal shows a definite change of mood even when the stimulation has stopped. A cat that was peaceful before the operation can react after stimulation with noises, as a phonetic threatening gesture, to the mere extension of the hand.

A deeper insight into the play of mental forces is given by the fact that the affective defense reaction leads to a behavior that seems to be opposite to an attack; the animal seems to get out of a dangerous situation by fleeing. This alternative, however, is no contradiction but rather gives an experimental contribution to an understanding of the so-called polarity of feelings. In the concrete case, it seems that by stimulation of moderate degree, evidently particularly in the marginal region of the defense zone, the cat is led to looking around (Hunsperger, 1956; Roberts, 1958). If she sees a way out, she immediately jumps off the experimental table and tries to reach safety in a corner or underneath an object. If there is no way out, she chooses another reaction that promises protection; she opposes the enemy and tries to avoid the danger by threatening gestures or swiftly executed attack. Thus, one behavior as well as the other is in the final analysis due to the same motive, namely, to the tension of being threatened in her existence. As we said, it is partly due to external circumstances which variant the cat will choose—perhaps the so-called skip reaction can be understood in a similar way. Externally instinctive behavior is blocked and a specific tension spread out, goes particularly to a deeper layer and from there is discharged in a different direction. To explain the motivation of the protective behavior by moods is also supported by experimnts of comparative psychophysiology. We have in mind here accounts by von Holst and von St. Paul (1960). In a lecture series, only the summary of which has so far appeared, they show that essentially there is unequivocal accord between their observations on cocks and our own experience with cats. The authors who have just been cited interpret their observations also in the sense that by electrical stimulation images are activated to which the animals react correctly.[1]

If we think about it more closely, we cannot expect anything but a close correspondence between behaviors that are brought about artificially through cerebral stimuli and those which are brought about naturally. If only the electrodes hit the proper spot, the neuronal elements of the specific centers can after all, once they are stimulated above threshold, only answer by excitation or inhibition, but are unable to distinguish between the qualities which stimulate them.

The findings that have just been referred to make us want to hear more about the localization of the stimuli. To this end, the histological investigation of the brain furnishes the orientation. This shows first of all an area in the diencephalon from which active loci extended into the midbrain (Hess and Brügger, 1943a). More detailed observations that were especially directed towards the syndrome of rage by Hunsperger (1956) and de Molina and Hunsperger (1959) have shown with all desirable clarity that in the midbrain too there is a

[1] Private communication from E. von Holst.

circumscribed region from which active defense reactions or the fleeing reaction can be elicited. Furthermore, we found points with the same effect which show a continuity between the two areas.

A further finding of these authors has to do with the connection by the stria terminalis of the diencephalo-mesencephalic system with the nucleus amygdalae, which is in the endbrain. On the basis of research by other authors, this leads still further. We are thinking here of results that have been particularly stressed by MacLean. We are dealing here with the functional importance of a phylogenetically old part of the endbrain that in its whole extent has been called the limbic system (MacLean, 1957, 1958a). By MacLean, this formation has been called the visceral brain and has been related to emotional behavior (MacLean, 1949). The experimental results further show that within the limbic system, not all parts are functionally of the same value. In the fronto-temporal part, there are mechanisms that play a role in food intake—for instance, sniffing, licking, biting, chewing, gagging, and vomiting (MacLean and Delgado, 1953). From other parts effects are produced that have to be considered as components of the affective defense or attack reactions. Neuro-endocrine symptoms also occur.

In this respect, activation of moods and their co-ordinated expressions are apparently closely related to parts of the septum, to the hippocampus and to the cingular gyrus. But the relations are somewhat complex, perhaps in the sense of polar opposites, as has been discussed in the first part. As experimental proof, we can point to the behavior of those monkeys which, after a lesion of the anterior cingular area, showed a complete change of their spontaneous behavior. Aggressive monkeys became extremely tame after the operation, while fearful monkeys lost the anxiety that they showed before the operation (Glees et al., 1950a). The changes are, according to Glees, partly the same as those found by workers in the United States (Smith, 1945; Ward, 1948). The anatomical investigation of Marchi preparations showed connections of the cingular gyrus with the anterior nucleus of the thalamus and with the cortex of the frontal lobe. The attempt to recognize an over-all plan of organization in the whole symptomatology led MacLean (1958b) to distinguish, among the functions that can be localized, between those that affect the survival of the species and those that affect the survival of the individual. How far this can be upheld will have to be shown in larger material. In the meantime, the findings after stimulation in the mesencephalon and diencephalon seem to show us that the limbic system plays the role of a mediator in the vertical neural organization; it transmits experiences that have an emotional component from the highest functional plane to the brain stem and from there to the effectors of the vegetative and the animal system. The pattern that develops out of the large number of stimulation experiments of MacLean and his co-workers and also out of the electrophysiological studies of P. Gloor (1955) on the cat is valid not only for the effect on the peripheral apparatus, but also for mental motivations and for these particularly as the experimental findings that we will talk about later seem to suggest.

Among the results of the stimulation experiments, one finds the statement that the affective defense can also be obtained by stimulation in the region of the cerebellum (Zanchetti and Zoccolini, 1954). When we test the technique used by these authors, we find that these experiments were made on cats who had previously been deprived of their cerebral hemispheres. Such prepared animals have, however, as we will see in a moment, an accentuated inclination to get into a rage. Unspecific stimuli even of small intensity are enough to produce such an emotive manifestation. Considering the connections between the cerebellum and the brain stem, we may

57

therefore assume that the observations of Zanchetti and Zoccolini are of indirectly projected effects and that the cerebellum cannot be considered the carrier of emotional contents of consciousness.

If we now consider the results of extirpation of the cerebral hemispheres, we find very detailed observations. The dog without an endbrain who is awake behaves as though the protective manifestation had lost its inhibition through lack of the endbrain (Goltz, 1892; Rothmann, 1923). Even after a small stimulus, for instance, touching him somewhere on the skin, the animal reacts by assuming a position of attack exactly as a normal animal would when irate or enraged. The cat without an endbrain also shows this increased readiness to be on the defensive with all its power, as when it comes together with other cats. (Bard, 1934; Bard and Rioch, 1937). That they do not attack a specific goal should be mentioned and this is understandable, because after all they cannot orient themselves optically. The increased tendency to expressions of rage on the part of decorticated dogs and cats has been shown by Woodworth and Sherrington (1904) and also by Cannon (1929). The experimenters talk of sham rage. In all likelihood, they chose this term because of the corticocentric ideas about relations between consciousness and brain that at that time were still prevalent. The stimulation experiments that have been mentioned above correct this idea and confirm a suppressive influence of the cortex on organizing dispositions at a hierarchically lower level.

If we further test the results of our experiments to stimulate the thalamus, we come across the drive to eat (Brügger, 1943; Hess, 1954a; Hess, 1956). It was expressed by a cat which formerly paid no attention to a bowl of milk or a piece of meat that was on the table. In immediate connection with the stimulation, it developed such a positive interest for these objects that it went to them with obvious greediness and ate or drank. This specific drive can be so strong that even objects that cannot be used for nourishment are taken up by the cat and gnawed at. A parallel to this behavior is the bulimia that occurs in psychiatric patients. For this reason, these constatations are also of importance for the psychopathologist; they show the value for psychiatry of experimental analyses of the brain.

What motivates the search for food, and what causes the desire to eat? Under normal conditions, the specific drive is due to a feeling of hunger, or in other words to a content of consciousness that is defined by its effect. If after our own experience we see how another man also strives for nourishment and when he has it, devours it with definite greediness, we do not doubt that he, too, acts under the influence of a high degree of hunger. An analogous reason can be assumed if our dog, driven by hunger, goes to his dish of food and sates himself. In free-living animals, we observe how, apart from the endogenous motive, which is the primary agent, exogenous factors also play a role. In this case, olfactory, acoustic, or visual sensations play a role, according to the specific constitution of the animal. Corresponding sensations lead to a search for nourishment or to eating. Other sensations suppress this desire if the sensory organs receive stimuli which are interpreted as danger signals and thus lead to caution or anxiety.

The function of the endogenous feeling of hunger and the evaluation of the visual, acoustic, olfactory, and gustatory impressions make impossible the direct transference of stimuli to the central representations of the muscles that are used in searching for nourishment and in eating. We have to postulate the working over of the various stimuli if there is to be a behavior that is in accord with the situation as a whole.

About the endogenous drive to take up solid food and liquid, one is informed by the impressive effect of well-planned experiments. Normally, hunger is elicited by lack of nutrients offered by the blood to central receptors. The diminution of sugar by insulin proves this. Parallel to it and still more precise is the central stimulation of water intake elicited by injection of hypertonic salt solutions into the hypothalamus (Andersson, 1953). The direct consequence of this operation is the overloading of the intercellular fluid with salts equivalent to a specific hypertension in the diencephalic structures. The result of such a state is a behavior which normally will decrease the concentraton of salts, as drinking of water. That this behavior is really called for by these experiments was shown in goats. The massive intake of water is an indication that the animal has been driven to it. The agent in the physiological pattern is the thirst which also must be assumed the sole agent in the case we have just described. Confirmation of the diencephalic origin is given by electrical stimulation that is supplanted by the histological confirmation of the positive stimulation point (Andersson and McCann, 1955). In this case, too, a large amount of water is immediately taken up. That the need for water is the corresponding feeling, that is to say, that the thirst is the leading motive is shown in a more sophisticated experiment. By letting goats go for a long time without water, Andersson made them thirsty in a normal manner and then he trained them to go over a staircase to a water vat from which they could slake their thirst. However, they were here given only a certain insufficient amount of water. To get a new ration of water, after emptying the vat, the goats had to go down the staircase and then up once more where they could drink the next water ration that had been put out in the meantime. When the training had been completed, the stimulation experiment that has been described was performed. It was shown that the goats, after stimulation of the thirst region, went up to the vat even if they had had enough to drink previously (Andersson and Wyrwicka, 1957). This behavior is a sure sign that by diencephalic stimulation, a specific feeling is evoked corresponding to the one that comes about if the animal has remained without water for several days and therefore is thirsty. In the stimulation experiments, this feeling was so strong under certain circumstances that even water that had been denatured to a certain extent by a bitter substance, salt, or acid was swallowed. In central polydipsia in man, a neuropathological condition, we find a confirmation of these assumptions because the patient tells us that he is tormented by an unquenchable thirst and therefore tries to get fluid in all possible ways.

By interpreting the endogenous drive to take up solids and liquids as due to analogous motives, we supplement the results of the thirst experiments by giving an account of other investigations that involve the stimulation of the eating drive. Here we also have the result of central stimulation and of circumscribed lesions. The results lead to the idea that the induced behavior is due to antagonistic forces in which the destruction of one gives rise to a heightened effectiveness of the other. Bilateral extirpation, according to the place where the extirpation was performed, could make the animal take up abnormally large amounts of food, while after lesions in the neighborhood, the intake of food is diminished. In the former case, the result is obesity (Hetherington and Ranson, 1940; Hess, 1954a); in the latter case, profound cachexia (Anand and Brobeck, 1951).

The experimental obesity is of particular interest because it shows that nourishment taken in is made use of by the intestinal tract and that the assimilated material is stored in the physiological depots. In the sense of a direct causal connection, one may expect that the increased intake may stimulate the metabolism so that the excess is got rid of. Since this is not the case and the metabolism, on the contrary, goes below the norm (Brooks, Marine, and Lambert, 1946), one has to conclude that the change caused by the operation works on all the members of the chain in the same direction, that is to say, from the drive to take up the nourishment to the final taking possession by the proper places of the body. It is consonant with this idea that in cases in which nourishment is declined, in spite of extreme cachexia, no desire to eat comes about and the increasing loss of substance does not lead to the behavior that normally, by intensifying the hunger drive, leads to a compensation of the losses by an energetic search for food. In summary, the agent that acts as a content of consciousness that keeps the individual on an even keel in the sector of nourishment corresponds to a functional organization that, like the other parts of the whole system, has to be looked for in the brain stem. It appears to us that this consequence is not only of psychophysiological interest, but also clinically important and makes a remarkable contribution to psychosomatic medicine.

Still clearer insight into the governing function of certain contents of consciousness come from training experiments. Rats are made hungry by not being fed and then are trained for a certain task. When they press a lever, they will get a ration of kernels to be eaten. The animals learn by prolonged experience what first happens only by chance. After a certain time, they learned to give themselves nourishment by purposely pressing the lever and they ate extensively. They had learned the effect of the lever and used this experience in the search for food. Subsequently, these experiments have been still further improved (Miller, 1957). The trained rats were first allowed to eat enough and then their behavior toward the food lever was watched, on the one side uninfluenced, on the other side after electrical stimulation of the hypothalamus. In the latter case, the lever was used many times more often than nomal. This activation shows conclusively that stimulation of the hypothalamus has the same effect as hunger. Finally, the experiments were still further refined by training the rats to go in case of thirst to a bowl of water, in cease of hunger to a container of solid food that was in another part of the cage, and thus to quench their thirst or sate themselves. The two vessels were coverd by trap doors. In the subsequent stimulation experiments it was shown that the feeding place was approached more often than the watering place if the stimulating electrode was in such a place that the stimulations led to the intake of food. Considering the results, the animals showed on one side the effect of their experience and on the other side the correlaton between certain behaviors with certain circumscribed areas of the hypothalamus. This interpretation is made still more certain by the experiments with goats (Andersson, Jewell, and Larson, 1958) that led to the same results.

An experimental finding should be mentioned that confirms the direction of certain behaviors by neuronal dispositions in the hypothalamus. It concerns the release of continuous autostimulation (Olds and Milner, 1954). The experimental animal (rat) is in a cage that contains a lever which, when activated, leads to a closing of a circuit with a stimulating electrode. Here, too, the stimulation is at first merely incidental, for instance when the rat goes around in the cage and by chance touches the lever. Eventually this leads either to an increase or to a definite avoidance of the lever, just as in training it leads to either reward or punishment. This result of autostimulation can be understood best by assuming that stimulation, when the electrode is properly placed, leads to a positive feeling tone. This leads to an increased use of the lever. In negative feeling tones, such as pain, the animal will, according to his experience, avoid touching the lever in the same way as the "burnt child" avoids fire. The induction of this or that behavior leads in one case as well as in the other to a certain feeling tone which is connected with the memory of the conditions under which it happened. This demonstrates the function of contents of consciousness. This interpretation does not exclude that in continuous autostimulation we gradually reach the point of an addiction (Jung, 1958). While it still develops, however, one has to assume that the reaction that is chosen between two possibilities is the manifestation of certain contents of conscousness.

After having described these experimental findings and their order according to subjective effects, we now tackle the question to which regions they are related. Accordingly, we first will talk about the localization of the stimuli that are responsible for this or that effect. According to our own stimulation experiments, we find for the drive to eat a region just behind the diencephalic area of affective avoidance and partly coextensive with it (Brügger, 1943). A closer definition will be possible when we have still more complete observations about the structural correlation of the drive to eat and to drink. In order to achieve that we need still further work, which of course has to include the histological investigation of the experimental brains. So far, evidently, the findings of American authors show that the stimuli which lead to thirst are close to the area in which our hunger points lie when we put them into their brain sections. From our own experience we feel that in order to be sure in this respect, there needs to be a great extension of the experiments.

If one supplements these findings of the stimulation of the brain stem by observations of dogs (Goltz, 1892; Rothmann, 1923) and cats (Dusser de Barenne, 1920) which have been made after extirpation of the endbrain, we see corroboration of the importance of the brain stem for the regulation of intake of food and fluids. Here, too, indications are not lacking that impulses which lead to intake of food are connected with the subjective feelings. This is shown, for instance, by the dog without an endbrain who, after a long pause in eating, becomes increasingly restless but shows by certain movements of the jaws and tongue what this restlessness is due to.

Further hints for subjective motivation that is due to structures in the brain stem, particularly the diencephalon, is given by the activation of the drive to clean oneself. This, too, can be produced by electrical stimulation of the diencephalon (Hess and Meyer, 1956). Simple licking is not important for an evaluation of this comparatively rare effect that seemingly has the character of an automatism. In caring for the skin, there is a systematic behavior in which all parts of the body that can be reached are taken care of one after the other and are treated with different intensity, according to their place. The change in the part of the skin that is to be worked on is probably controlled by species and place-specific sensations apart from the automatic movements of licking. We have this impression even where parts of the body are cared for that cannot be reached directly by the tongue. We are thinking here of the face. Apart from the perioral parts, the cat uses his forepaw in such a way that he licks it first and then washes his face with this instrument. The observations of the dog and the cat without the endbrain (Goltz, 1892; Rothmann, 1923; Bard and Rioch, 1937) are well in accord with the observations on cats whose diencephalon was stimulated. That this happens less energetically than in a normal animal shows that the endbrain helps in this performance. It belongs to the topic of innate cleanliness that the animals avoid dirtying themselves by defecation and micturition. The positions typical for these activities are often brought about by stimulation of the hypothalamus and, with a still greater certainty, by stimulation of the septal region (Hess and Brügger, 1943b). The cat is generally very long in "position," that is to say, about half a minute, until the pressing occurs which then leads to extrusion of the excrement. The imminent voiding is also foreshadowed. The cat becomes restless, walks around, and tries to find a place where she can go into position and then urinate in the normal manner. These signs which allow the observer to guess at what will come next, are indications that the animal, after the beginning of stimulation, experiences a wish to defecate or micturate and is stimulated by the specific contents of consciousness to a behavior which, as we said, avoids soiling itself. This interpretation has to be made more precise, however. We have to reckon with the possibility that the effective electrode has met fibers that ascend from the wall of the bladder or the rectum and thus induce in the animal the desire to defecate or micturate; in other words, that the peripheral situation is reproduced in consciousness. In this case, the experiment would simply imitate the effects of an adequate peripheral stimulus and would not directly hit the substrate that is a carrier of the subjective impressions. Localization of the stimuli would thus show the course of those afferent fibers that, under physiological conditions, would lead to the specific feeling to which the cat answers with the reactions that we have described. According to our experiences, the greatest number of elements that indicate the afferent stimuli to the carriers of specific feelings, and thus co-ordinate the synergism of the effectors, are situated in the septum pellucidum.

Finally, it is of interest whether diencephalic stimulation experiments produce behaviors that can be brought in connection with contents of consciousness in the sphere of sexuality. In some experiments, stimulus-bound behavior was observed which also becomes manifest physiologically in connection with sexual excitement. This is a rhythmic lifting and putting down of the paws, alternating between right and left, the so-called stepping, and also, a frequently repeated touching of the head and side of the body on objects, for instance, the legs of observers (Meyer and Hess, 1957). As a further criterion, there is a certain kind of phonation. For complete evaluation of this accoustic expression, registering of the tones, which at the time of the experiment was not yet possible, parallel to cinematographic registration, would have given the desired certainty.

As far as the male animal (Saimiri sciureus) is concerned, erection was observed during diencephalic stimulation (MacLean, Ploog, and Robinson, 1960). This effect, too, can be induced by tactile stimulations of the penis when the animal is ready for sexual discharges. If ejaculation actually occurred, it would be analogous to the experience of micturition or defecation described above. Since, in all these cases, a lumbar co-ordination center has the last word and under given circumstances works reflexly, it stands to reason, then, that the central effect is related to the superordinated part of the sexual system, whose functioning is normally connected with the sexual content of consciousness.

Apart from these experiments, we also have to pay attention to the findings of Bard. This experimenter has studied in detail the behavior, particularly in respect to sexual excitation, of cats whose endbrain had been surgically removed (Bard, 1940). Tramping of the hind legs, walking around trying to find tactile stimuli, and turning around, according to the normal behavior of the sexually excited female cat, were observed. Phonetic expressions also occurred, just as in the cat with intact brain that is ready for coitus. Thus it is confirmed that to get the sexually oriented behavior the brain stem is sufficient, just as in activation of the behavior in thirst and hunger, where we thought it likely that these states are experienced as specific tensions.

As far as the more exact localization of the structures that are important for sexual excitation is concerned, observations with diathermic destruction of the tuber cinereum in cats and rats gives some hints (Bustamente, Spatz, and Weisschedel, 1942; Bustamente, 1943). If one destroys the tuber cinereum, the drive to make contact with an individual of the other sex is abolished. Of course, the abolishment of libido may be

67

secondary because after this operation the sexual glands may degenerate. Therefore, a hormonal component is taken away and with it one of the conditions of specific functional readiness. A direct neuronal component is, however, not excluded and remains at any rate for discussion.

Further remarkable observations have been made as a consequence of bilateral extirpation of the temporal lobes with excision of the amygdalae (Bucy and Klüver, 1955; Klüver and Bucy, 1938; Klüver, 1952). Deficiency symptoms are in such cases a definite change of the emotional character, in the sense of an accentuated oral control associated with hypersexuality; furthermore, there was a disturbance in taking care of the young where normally a subjective control has to be assumed.

The experiments that have been described so far are put on a broader basis by new results in behavioral sciences in the sense of comparative psychophysiology (von Holst, 1957; von Holst and von St. Paul, 1960). As experimental animals, these authors use cocks and hens. Finely graded electric stimuli were applied to the region of the basal ganglia. In the evaluation of the symptoms and syndromes that appeared, von Holst differentiates between effects of a simple nature such as sitting down, getting up, and cleaning the feathers. The last is obviously to be equated with the taking care of the hairs in our own experiments in cats after stimulation of the between brain (p. 66). In other cases and under different conditions von Holst also observed, as we did in cats, drives, e.g., to defend oneself or to flee. A concrete example of the first effect is the aimed attack at a stuffed polecat or at the face of the caretaker who is within reach. The cock, just like the cat, will make a visual connection with the electrically induced mood to attack in such a way that the most accessible object becomes an enemy. Furthermore, behaviors were found that correspond to those that are evoked under physiological conditions by hunger. In other experiments, the animals behave under an electrical stimulus as in wooing or in the drive to execute the marital dance, in finding food in the same way as our cats, or in the drive to drink, just like Andersson's goats.

As far as the localization of the stimulus that is responsible for this or that effect is concernd, von Holst keeps to measurements when he places the electrodes. He is led to say that one and the same reaction can be brought about from different loci and that from the same locus different reactions can be elicited by varying the strength of the stimulus. This corresponds to our own experiences that are based on the histological control of the stimulus loci that have the same effect. If von Holst has, under certain circumstances, observed behavior after central stimulation that is analogous to conflicts of drives, this corresponds to the example in which the cat is in conflict between defense by attack and by the tendency to flee (Hunsperger, 1956).

If one summarizes these experimental findings, the results in birds and mammals are amazingly similar, at least insofar as they concern behavior that is in direct connection with the maintenance of the individual, corresponds to the same needs, and contains hints of a correspondence of the functional organization of the brains and carriers of the excitatory processes that become manifest contents of consciousness.

In the behaviors that are due to drives, we must also include certain feelings and moods of a higher order which become manifest in a typical manner. If one wants to find here connections with certain formations of the brain, one will use experiences that have been made during operations by brain surgeons. Exact knowledge is, at the moment, however, quite sparse. All the more valuable are positive findings as they have become available recently through a pooling of research by a brain surgeon and a brain anatomist (Hassler

69

and Riechert, 1961). In the concrete case, it has to do with laughing after electric stimulation of the diencephalon. More exactly, it was described by the first author in this way: during stereotactic operations for hyperkinesis or Parkinsonism in awake, co-operative patients, a smile, and sometimes a definite laughing can be produced and reproduced by electric stimulation. If the patient is asked before repeating the stimulation not to laugh, he nonetheless cannot suppress it. Afterward, he will say that when the stimulation occurred, everything seemed to be funny or that the same amusing situation in his former life came into his mind. One has to conclude, therefore, that the stimulation does not directly affect the facial musculature, which has to be co-ordinated for laughing but is determined as an objective expression of certain contents of consciousness. As far as the part of the brain is concerned, one can only consider the place where the electrodes are introduced. A large number of patients reacted in the manner that has been described and nine per cent of these did so repeatedly. This effect can be produced from the inner margin of the ventral oral nucleus of the thalamus where it borders on the medial lamella.[2] The laughing effect is not to be correlated with the neurons of the oral ventral nucleus itself, which projects to the motor cortex, but to the stimulation of fibers of passage from the unspecific nuclei of the thalamus to other parts of the basal ganglia. Apart from this localization, laughing or smiling and a good mood has also been found after stimulaton of the pallidum; here, however, in only three and one-half per cent of all cases.

If we now try to be more precise about the correlations between structural organizaton and the character of drive-

[2] TRANSLATOR'S NOTE.—This has been corrected from the German sentence following a correspondence with Dr. K. Akert, who got in touch with Professor Hess himself. I wish to thank both of them once more for their co-operation.

induced behavior connected with subjective experience, we find from the histologically controlled cat's brains that the ergo-tropic (so-called sympathicotonic) moods that lead to a certain goal-directed drive are found more in the posterior parts of the hypothalamus, while the endophylactic-protective, the so-called vagotonic, reactions are more closely related to the anterior parts of the hypothalamus. Since in the hypothalamus we also find regulatory structures of the vegetativum, the co-ordination of extraverted behavior on the one side and of the activity and reactivity of various vegetative organs and organ groups on the other side is easily understood, and so is the correlation between psychic contents and vegetative symptoms.

Following the example of affective defense reactions, we will mention a few facts about the connections between certain moods and feeling tones on the one side and the response of certain vegetative organs and organ groups on the other side. The point is whether these correlations have a specific character. This is, for instance, the case when in rage the blood goes to the head and the emotion becomes clear to the outsider by a red face. Evidently, we have here to do with an involuntary but nonetheless effective component of human threatening posture. The manifest behavior is directed toward physical activity. It is also true that in man as well as in the stimulated cat the pupils and the palpebral fissure become much wider. The increase of the heart rate and the rise of blood pressure is part of the same syndrome, as is the increase of the rate of respiration. As far as this symptom is concerned, the psychic influence is shown by the fact that in man an activation of respiration can occur if he knows that he will be doing physical work and that the person who is put into an ergometer (Krogh and Lindhard, 1913) increases his respiration when he merely thinks that he does hard work but actually does only minimal work or none at all. The importance of this mental component seems to be that during the actual work of the body, it helps the purely somatic regulations by lowering the threshold for lack of CO_2 or O_2.

Another case of specific connections between a certain mood and the vegetative reactions is seen in the proverbial contraction of the bladder musculature and the activation of the peristalsis of the intestine, frequently concomitant with an increase in perspiration, which occur when a person is afraid. This can hardly be considered as a goal-directed projection of a specific mood. However, obviously, these symptoms belong to a trophotropic function that is directed toward a decrease of tension. The response of the vegetative effectors can be understood as an irradiation limited to this system. The same may be true of the increase of secretion of urine which is due to a tense expectation of an important decision that is about to occur.

Specific connections can be observed when blushing occurs. This vasomotor effect can be considered a mute language that shows the mood and thereby, seen in a larger frame, gives informaton to the partner better than a spoken word. The connection between deep mourning and other injuries of the personality with the secretion of tears is also clear. On the other hand, the lacrimal gland responds to a certain extent also to great joy, particularly in connection with unrestricted laughter. This needs an unusually large emotion so that one has to think in this case of an all-embracing, unspecific irradiation. The vegetative reaction to anger is well known. As everybody knows from himself, the secretory function of the glands of the digestive system, for instance, the secretion of the oral saliva no less than the secretion of the juices of the stomach, is inhibited. Another part of this effect that shows in the activity of the glands is the inhibition of the motor function of the intestine. In this case, there is a mutual connection between the trophotropic and the ergotropic system. The inhibition of the former is due to the fact that it is centrally connected with an activation of the latter (Hess, 1948b, p. 198). This centrally organized reciprocal induction of the antagonists maintains and accentuates the effect of a change in mood.

If one goes further afield among the connections that are now being discussed, one finds that there are large differences from individual to individual, on the one side as a consequence of different dispositions, on the other side due to the different momentary readiness of various vegetative organs, partly in connection with the immediate history of their use. Of importance, apart from the momentary feelings and moods, are those tones of feeling that are anchored in the experience of an individual and become reactivated when certain things are remembered.

If we summarize the various hints and the results of a still larger analysis of the connections between moods and their expression, then a first survey will already make it clear that an experience that has a feeling tone rarely mobilizes one organ alone but generally a whole group of organs. It depends largely on the intensity of the feeling tone whether a specific influence is limited to one functional system or whether the stimulus will spread out and under certain circumstances will break through the limits of organic order and irradiate into other systems. Under certain circumstances, very strong emotions will make themselves felt in the whole vegetativum as an unco-ordinated mental upheaval.

A particular importance is attached to mutual psychosomatic relations in those cases in which activation or suppression becomes conscious only after the fact. In this way, the primary mood is intensified so that the influence on the vegetativum is increased. Thus the feeling becomes an intensive experience, not least because of the help of the hormonal system (Cannon, 1929). That disturbances in the somatic expression of moods having regard to the physiological basis of the connections are apt to elaborate the picture which has been sketched may be mentioned at the end of this discussion.

VOLUNTARY MOVEMENTS AS FUNCTIONAL DOCUMENTATION OF CEREBRAL ORGANIZATION

A presupposition for making a goal-directed voluntary movement is a defined position from which to start. In the case of the eyes, one talks of a primary position with the gaze straight forward. From this position one looks sideways, upward, downward, or in an oblique direction, according to the relative position between the object and the eyes. For the head and body, the primary position is the upright posture, from which we go to positions that are proper to certain functions. We have seen such movements in our cats as indirect effects, for instance, when they go from sleeping to wakefulness after an awakening stimulus. The animal gradually gets up from lying down, in order to get active contact with the surroundings and, on the proper occasion, to do something.

If we go from the position of eyes, head, and body and of the extremities and facial musculature over to the co-ordinated movements directed to certain effects, here, too, it is best to go from simple to more complex behaviors. In any case, the bio-motoric must be clear as a physical phenomenon. From this point of view, one has to keep in mind that the final result of any motor activity is a composition of forces that are co-ordinated simultaneously and successively. The psychomotor innervation, too, has to take that into account in order to organize a corresponding pattern of impulses. One has to keep in mind that in longer-lasting activity, the achievement becomes more complicated insofar as during movement the equilibrium of head, body, and members will shift because they change their position. Correspondingly, forces have to be used in different combinations and in different strengths from one phase to the other. The certainty with which we hit our goal demonstrates that this actually happens and happens, moreover, unconsciously and automatically. Another physical law which has to be taken into account in motor innervation is that of the so-called forces of reaction. Whenever a movement is begun, is inhibited, or changes its direction, forces spring up that are quantitatively of the same amount but act in opposite directions. In the mechanical model, such as the gun or rifle, one sees or feels them as recoil. The same thing happens if we start a voluntary movement, although we do not know it. The movement would, without doubt, go in the wrong direction if these reactive forces were not taken into account at every step. The execution of a voluntary movement shows that this, too, is completely automatic.

The forces of gravitation are to be reckoned with. In point of fact, in shaping the movement for a certain goal, gravitation plays a not inconsiderable role and demands a certain organization from the innervation. These are fulfilled just like the other components, without our becoming conscious of them. By all these forces acting together, we arrive at a dynamic basis for our goal-directed voluntary movement, which becomes a movement guided by the will even if it takes a long time. As far as the neuronal dispositions are concerned, which organize these forces, numerous observations give closer information. First of all, we have in mind the reflex mobilization by the lower parts of the brain stem which was shown experimentally by Magnus and his co-workers (Magnus, 1924). The corresponding neuronal apparatus is, however, under the guidance of a mechanism which is predominantly situated in the diencephalon. It is a fact that after electrical stimulation of this part of the brain in definite places one can see the effect of forces that are projected and combined according to the principle of the parallelogram of forces. Here, too, the guidance has partly the character of reflexes, namely, under the influence of the vestibular apparatus to which proprioceptive afferents are added. Destroying the responsible substrate shows that in wakefulness this substrate is under a constant tonus and that the keeping of any position means continuous dynamic equilibrium, or a sequence of consecutive equilibria in the sense of correcting movements. However, strong disturbances that are beyond the effectiveness of these automatisms get into consciousness and one looks around for a support to which one can hold on so that one can insure the stance voluntarily. The motivation of this behavior is particularly convincing if one anticipates a disturbance of the stance and takes measures to meet it successfully. Finally, we have also to take into account in this connection the facial expression as an equilibrium of the muscular forces that determine it. As a stance it is, according to experimental findings, automatically insured; that is to say, as a position of origin from which those psychomotor innervations are developed that give expression to moods and feelings. But here, too, voluntary innervation may overrule the automatic distribution of the tonus and may adjust to external situations.

If we try to summarize our picture of the forces in space and time which develop a voluntary goal-directed activity, it becomes noticeable how many combinations of impulses can be given out without a conscious effort. Thus, attention can be concentrated on the end and, in longer-lasting actions, also on important partial goals.

After this survey of the presuppositions of a voluntary action whose central organization will lead to a desired goal, a few examples will be given that enlarge and reinforce experimentally the relations that have been described.

The simplest case that has been examined in detail is that of a fish waiting for a prey that assumes the fixed position proper to going quickly forward and that has to compensate for the gravitational force. An opportunity to observe the movement of the fins which insure this position is given by the rainbow trout, which can easily be kept in large aquaria. This fish also demonstrates in an impressive manner its behavior during the reaction of grabbing if a prey, for instance a worm, is brought into view. The experimental analysis by K. Akert (1949) has shown the following. When diathermically circumscript parts at the margin of the retina of one eye have been destroyed (a place where moving objects in the periphery of the visual field are optically projected), it was shown by degeneration that this retinal place projects to the surface of the opposite tectum opticum of the midbrain. Thus, stimulation of photoreceptors of the retina are transmitted to this part of the central nervous system.

A second assumption concerns the connection between the tectum opticum and the somatomotor apparatus. If elements on the surface of this formation are stimulated, muscular forces are activated in a well-defined manner. These are first of all movements of the eye and secondly propulsion of the body. Thus a large co-ordination of motor effectors becomes manifest. The effect of this is to reach a visually perceived goal. The whole corresponds to the behavior in which the experimental animal is first of all activated by a visually perceived object, then makes it a target, and then catches it. Stimulated by the drive to eat and directed by visual experience, it "wants" to catch the prey, principally in the same manner in which we ourselves, for instance, reach for a fruit that we like, first move toward it, and finally bring it to the mouth. We have to question such comparisons, however, and we would be more inclined to assume only a simple reflex in the fish. That the reaction of grasping the prey depends on exteroceptive influences does not altogether speak against this. On the other hand, there is no necessary reason to assume that in the fish, in spite of its comparatively simple organization of the brain, there is not a subjective movement involved, i.e., that after a conscious perception it does not decide or choose between possible behaviors and a "volition." Since we have no definite criteria, we leave the problems of psychomotor behavior and consciousness in lower vertebrates open. To correlate goal-directed reaction with cerebral organization is, however, unequivocal.

The next step of experimental control involves animals with higher central nervous systems in which the leading role of visual experience is more highly differentiated. Here one can refer to experiments with parrots (Kalischer, 1905). Kalischer has tested these birds, which are mentally remarkably gifted, in the one case for psychomotor abilities and in the other for the consequences of extirpation of certain parts of the brain. When investigating intact animals, he showed that they largely rely on their eyes to orient themselves about the topographic relations of themselves to objects in their surroundings and also about processes in the visual space itself. Following a genuine desire for information, the parrot looks here and there. The effects of the external muscles of the eye are helped by synergistic combinations with muscles which determine the position and the movements of the head. In the extirpation experiments, it has been shown that the visually induced movements are co-ordinated with two different parts of the brain. The one corresponds to the beak zone. It embraces those parts of the visual field which have to do with the control and the target of picking up objects. When the anterior quadrigeminal bodies are removed, the animal is no longer able to execute the movements of conversions which are necessary to fix the object in the beak zone. The animal can still react to experiences that are given in a part of the visual field which comprises larger areas outside of the beak zone. If the epistriatum, which belongs to the endbrain, is taken away, the animal does not respond any more to optical impressions that reach the lateral or posterior part of the visual field.

In the interpretation of the results of the experiment, it is not quite certain whether the lack of reaction induced by vision is due to the fact that the animal really does not see any more or whether the lesion has prevented the formulation of the adequate motor response, that is to say, a corresponding shift of gaze. If one wants any further material to evaluate this alternative, one can go back to experiments which use symptoms of emotional upheaval. To give expression to these, as we said, the parrot is very well equipped by the response of vegetatively innervated organs whose activity can be observed. This is particularly true of the change in the pupillary diameter in constant light, of the width of the pupillary fissure with the nictatating membrane, and also of the position of the feathers, all of which make the mood very clear. Unfortunately, we do not know enough today, so we cannot answer the questions that we discussed. To get the necessary material, by further experiments, would be a gratifying task which can be achieved by basing one's conclusions on the one hand on the described experiences, and on the other hand on one's own observations.

We shall now go from the bird to a mammal in which the ocular movements also play a great role; protocols, movies, and brain sections of cats are available in great amount (Hess, 1954a, 1956). The analysis of the motor expressions produced from the diencephalon furnishes us with criteria which make a more detailed evaluation possible and show that the stimulation experiments, when critically evaluated with the necessary precautions, will give remarkable information. First of all, we think about cases in which the cat lowers the head or brings it above the normal position of equilibrium. It is very clear that these movements have nothing to do with volition, for the pulse frequency of the stimulation is reflected in the form of intermittent motor impulses. This shows that the stimulation goes immediately to fibers that are efferent and that the effect is similar to what one would find if one stimulated descending fibers and thus indirectly the motor neurons. It is quite different with movements of the eye which appear when near-threshold stimuli establish weak stimulation on the surface of the anterior quadrigeminal bodies. The cat reacts to this with co-ordinated movements of the head and eyes, exactly as though she noticed something in the lateral or superior part of the visual field, depending on the place where the electrode is applied. The eye movements have a smooth, fluid character, so that the effect must be related to a substrate which is central to the motor innervation system, to which it gives a series of impulses in a more frequent rhythm than its own. Without being able to exclude completely an automatism for the changeover to higher frequencies, one has to keep in mind that the electrical stimulation of the surface of the optic tectum has the same effect as though impulses are transmitted to this formation from the retina of an eye; thereby an eccentrically projected visual experience is produced. The anatomic relations at least are given, as direct connections of the periphery of the retina with the optic tectum which have also been shown in the cat (Hoessly, 1947). Thus it can be understood that in electrically induced movements of the eye, one has the expression of an active movement which is induced by certain contents of consciousness. In this case, the cat looks in the direction from which, under normal conditions, a visual experience emanates. Since after fixation of the head and eyes, this is kept so long as the tectal stimulation is not increased, a reflex mechanism can hardly be assumed, all the less so since it has been shown in dogs without an endbrain that for some time after the operation they will avoid obstacles in the room. A reduced ability to see is, of course, sufficient to account for this case, i.e., a loss of finer differentiation. A sufficient neuronal organization is developed in the mammal as in man in the occipital lobe from which, as is well known, stimulation also induces eye movements. Furthermore, experiments have shown that from these parts of the brain experience of light, even the experience of shapes and colors, can be brought into consciousness (Penfield and Rasmussen, 1950). As far as experience and oculomotor innervation are related in time, that is to say, coincide, we may interpret the former as subjective motivation for the latter.

Experiments in cats who can move around freely show another region that in all probability is connected with voluntary eye movements. It is the area cingularis of the frontal brain (Hess, 1948a). The eye movements that are produced from here are often so well expressed that the cat will look over her back straight to the rear. Remarkable here is the fixed gaze and also the long latency of thirty seconds or more. The last indicates that one has to do with a complicated process, with several relays of stimuli. Several influences might be in competition, including components from other than visual spheres and including memory. In this sense, one can also interpret the remarkably fast disappearance of the effect after repeated stimulations, which also is true under natural conditions when the same experiment is repeated over and over again. An important argument for assuming that the turning of the eyes elicited from the cingular area is connected with the contents of consciousness is given by the bilateral removal of this area. The animal that has just been operated on (the monkey) runs, in contrast to the normal animal, into obstacles that can be visually perceived (Schaltenbrand and Cobb, 1930). Thus, one gets the impression that after the operation the picture received by the visual system is no longer recognized, or at least not interpreted according to its content as an impediment.

Finally, those eye movements have to be taken into account which appear after stimulation of a comparatively circumscript region of the motor zone. An attempt to establish connections between these various observations, so that one has a survey of the whole system which leads from the exogenous stimulus in conjunction with an endogenous drive to co-ordinate eye movements, however, meets still unknown quantities, so that a complete elucidation is only possible in broader connections when other findings are taken into consideration.

A step in this direction is the analysis of the grasping reaction in which arm, hand, and fingers work synergistically and in which an individual gifted with a mind will take possession of a desirable object, such as fruit. A concrete example is a monkey who knows that in a box, the so-called problem box, there is some food (Glees, 1956; Glees et al., 1950b). This knowledge, in connection with a desire to eat the food, leads to an attempt by the anterior extremities which are adapted to finer movements to open the closed box. In the beginning, the whole process is simply a probing around. If a pattern of co-ordination leads by chance and repeatedly to success, the positive feeling tone leads to a fixation of this co-ordination. If the monkey goes on trying, manual dexterity is increased and the amount of time and of force is considerably reduced. Afterward, Glees and co-workers extirpated the comparatively circumscript region of the motor or precentral cortex, from which, before the operation, electric stimulation led to movements of the thumb. After extirpation, when the animal awakes from narcosis, the hand was at first in flaccid paralysis, as was to be expected, and the trained ability of the hand was lost. Gradually, as is also the rule after circumscript lesions in the motor zone, the paralysis spontaneously improved to a great extent so that the experimenters could again begin with the training and this was again crowned by success. Parallel with it, the repeated control with electrical stimulation showed that innervatory relations between elements in the immediate neighborhood of the extirpated region of the thumb had become established, and that now stimulation of elements which before the extirpation had not led to movements of the thumb now led to such movements. By the second training, therefore, structures are brought into the co-ordinated pattern of innervation that in the intact brain did not participate, either because they had a higher threshold or because they were suppressed by the more focal elements which were supraordinated to them. Carrying these experiments still further, it was shown that elements that remained after the first extirpation and which in the second training period become part of the innervation pattern could then no longer be functionally restored. These experiences lead to a number of remarkable consequences:

1. The voluntary behavior is primarily induced by a conscious goal.

2. Actual perceptions and memories which belong to them increase the tension, and thus lead in general to behavior that is directed towards an object.

3. A number of variants fulfill the function of trial and error.

4. The positive feeling tone of the proper and repeated chance leads to a pattern of co-ordination which then is reinforced and remembered.

5. Disturbances in this process of co-ordination to a certain extent evened out by shifting of the excitability of various elements; the functional deficit is compensated.

If one brings together all these facts in a directed voluntary action, one will decline the idea that the organization of a goal-directed motor activity is induced by a structurally localized "center" and directed by it in its course. On the other hand, the interpretation of the experimental observations is well founded that large parts of the brain work together, including components of the brain stem. The internal play of forces is so far not too well known. The result, as we know from ourselves, is experienced as a manifestation of a volition directed to a certain accomplishment. How the neuronal happenings become the contents of our consciousness is still another question. About this we can only say that both have to do with tensions and that we cannot understand them in the sense of causal connections.

After this, we should direct our attention to some other experimental findings. Among others we should mention the experience that by electrical stimulation, no effects are produced from the motor cortex which resemble voluntary movements. There are, furthermore, definite differences in the latent period (Liddell, 1954). Also, a certain motor effect elicited from the cortex can be reproduced after the cortex has been taken away when the stimulating electrode is directly in contact with the descending fibers (Bates, 1954). This finding is in accord with the fact that circumcision of a stimulation point does not change the effect—that there is no co-ordinated spread from the artificial stimulus. This has to be contrasted with the fact that derivations of action potentials from numerous electronic channels during a voluntarily executed movement of the thumb show a spread of the electrical potentials, so that one can construct a kind of figure from the curves which have been registered (Lilly and Cherry, 1954). These two findings look at first sight as though they contradicted each other. But before one draws this conclusion one has to investigate more closely. This is all the more necessary, as at the moment far too little is known about the correlation between stimulations which are applied for a certain effect and the pictures which we obtain as curves from the electrical potentials.

As far as the correlation of co-ordinated functions in the motor zone and their relation to contents of consciousness is concerned, we only know that electrical stimulation in the thumb region elicits not only movements but also sensations. The patient feels the necessity to move the thumb (Penfield and Rasmussen, 1950). One might think, therefore, that certain contents of consciousness are connected immediately with the activity of certain neuronal elements during motor action.

There are several reasons, however, why one rather has to do with the retrograde spread of excitation which mobilizes those formations from which the impulse to co-ordinated movement normally arises and which go to the cortical representation of the motor effectors. Such interpretation, posed as a question, at least shows a way in which an insight into the functional and integral organization of the brain may be deepened, including the correlation between neuronal formulations and the mental activity that goes with them.

A step in the direction of clearing up the motor co-ordination and localization of structures that contribute to it are experimental results which have been known for quite a while, but still are of interest in this connection. These are results of electrical stimulation in areas of the cortex that are immediately in front of the motor zone, in the so-called premotor region (Wyss, 1937, 1938; Wyss and Obrador, 1937). In experiments on monkeys, these authors showed that from this region large groups of muscles are brought into action. If one persists in stimulating for some time, other muscles are included in such a way that one obtains patterns of functions that correspond to the organization of goal-directed movement. Furthermore, the sequence of a cut which severs premotor and motor region show that both areas are closely connected with each other in the sense that the premotor zone acts on the motor zone. One thus obtains indications that in the former region there are neuronal dispositions that play an important role in the synergistic co-ordination of muscles into groups which are used in voluntary movement. However, so far we are not aware of any investigations confirming these findings which fit so well into our concept. On the other hand, one finds indications that Area 6 is not sufficiently well known as far as stimulations and extirpations or its fiber connections go (Woolsey et al., 1951; Travis, 1955a, 1955b). Thus, for a final evaluation of the results one has to wait for further investigations which take into account that voltage, frequency, and state of the animal are of great importance quite apart from the localization.

The stimulation experiments of O. A. M. Wyss are, aside from the hints which we have just discussed, of interest in other directions. These experiments show that stimulations in the premotor zone also activate components of the so-called extrapyramidal system. The importance of these observations is that at the same time that the goal-directed forces are brought into play, muscle reactions are brought about which give the body the necessary stance from phase to phase; in other words, which give the necessary dynamic basis for the action which is in process (cf. p. 75).

A third function is co-ordinated with the innervation patterns from the premotor zone. With the motor processes which are elicited from this region, there goes hand in hand an ergotropic or sympatheticotonic change in the experimental animal. The consequence is a bodily state in which, on the one side, the psychomotor apparatus can very easily be influenced and, on the other side, vegetative organs become activated which increase some of the motor effects. As far as the contents of consciousness are concerned, which could conceivably be elicited by stimulation of the premotor zone, there are no objective symptoms because a monkey cannot talk to us about them. It may be possible to answer this question if the neurosurgeon for diagnostic or therapeutic reasons has to stimulate this region. One will be very much interested in hearing about such findings. At the moment one has to be content with indirect indications, as they have been explained by the combination of stimulations, extirpations and the training method.

The picture which has so far been developed is added to by a behavior which shows how deeply and securely the drive to voluntary actions is anchored. In this direction point observations in which the monkey who has been trained to open a box to obtain food tries to achieve the same result after the learned movements have been lost. He uses other helps which are still intact, for instance the other hand and sometimes also the lips (Glees, 1956). Obviously, he wants to compensate for the functional defect as far as possible and relieve the existing tension by satisfying his desire.

Finally, let us consider certain experiences which were made in man, using language as a means of understanding. The observations confirm that in man certain forms of voluntary movements presuppose the integrity of the precentral convolution (Penfield, 1954). Here the effects of an ablation are particularly seen in the loss of differentiated movements as they are developed only after the early stages of childhood. Partly or only very little disturbed are the primitive motor expressions which the baby can execute before he has acquired more complicated motor co-ordination by continuous practice. This is confirmed by the experience that at an early age a wound in the precentral gyrus has little or no effect on motor performance. Thus, one has to assume that in the processes of co-ordination, subcortical neural populations are involved, and therefore that the structural organization belongs to different levels. This follows also from careful ablation of the precentral convolution, because the motor functions which are lost on account of the operation are not restored to the same degree. An apparently complete ablation of the precentral convolution in the region of the arm leads first of all to a complete paralysis of this member. After a certain time, voluntary movements can again be executed, but only with the shoulder, the elbow, and the hand. Finely co-ordinated movements of the fingers are lost forever. This shows impressively that the co-ordination of a voluntary movement proceeds in steps in which the differentiation, as we have just said, plays an important role. The organization of psychodynamic effects in various steps is also shown by other experiences. A complete one-sided ablation of the region from which voluntary movements of the face are elicited leaves largely intact the musculature of the front and the muscles which close the eye. However, the voluntary control of other parts of the face is found wanting. For this the degree of differentiation of the innervation is probably important. The lips and their surroundings execute very finely organized movements without which speaking would be impossible.

One more experience in man should be mentioned. The relations between the peripheral somatomotor apparatus and its cortical representation show no principal differences when compared with more highly organized vertebrates. Penfield's constation underlines the importance of comparative physiology of the brain and of the mental manifestations of its functional organization.

To conclude the account of the cortical co-ordinatory function of the brain, we can adduce experiments that concern connections with subcortical structures. We have in mind findings that have been described in detail elsewhere. In the first place, it is important to look for criteria which allow us to draw a line between automatic and voluntary movements. Avoiding a too extensive treatment of this subject, we want to mention at least a few examples which show that conditions differ according to the plane in which a movement is executed. In the vertical, sagittal, and frontal planes, the motor effects elicited from the diencephalon reproduce at appropriate frequency of stimulations intermittent bouts of activity. In the horizontal plane, however, the movement is fluid, according to the locus which is stimulated, ipsi- or contraversive. The latency is much longer here; in ipsiversive movements at least one to three seconds, in contraversive movements fifteen seconds or more. The supposition is therefore well founded that particularly in the last case we have to do with a complicated process.

We are inclined to assume that an animal feels a tension along the axis of the body on the one side and therefore wants to correct the deviation back to straight posture, by a voluntary movement. Special features are found in the turning of the head, sometimes also of the anterior part of the body, as a consequence of a stimulus in a definite region. If one moves the head, which is obliquely turned, back to the normal position while the stimulus still goes on, the impeded rotation goes over to the eyes so that they are now turned obliquely. In this substituted function, we have an instance of subjective orientation in relation to the vertical. Probably guided by the organs of equilibrium, it happens reflexly. It is quite certain that a voluntary innervation can be excluded, because the cat cannot turn the eye around the axis of vision by voluntary effort any more than we can do it.

Finally, we have to take into account that regulation of the head-body position results under special circumstances from a combination of automatism and voluntary innervation. We invoke the latter, as we mentioned before, if outside forces lead to a strong deviation from the normal position. It even happens in man, as was mentioned before, that he anticipates a disturbance of equilibrium and invokes forces which will counterbalance the foreseen displacement. Here it is quite certain that the motivation can only be an expression of a certain content of consciousness, and therefore is mediated by voluntary innervations which are added to the automatic forces in a synergistic fashion.

THE FUNCTIONS OF SENSORY SYSTEMS

Of all the functions of the sensory system, one of the most elementary sensory experience is pain. It comes about, as we all know, when body tissues are wounded, frequently in very different fashions. Relatively well localized is the pain due to lesions by external forces, which appears fairly rapidly. There

89

is also another kind of pain which is more diffuse and much more sluggish in its course. A glance into the pathopsychophysiology shows that this pain is an almost constant concomitant of inflammation, which means that the threshold depends upon local conditions. Generally known is also its definite negative feeling tone which determines the protective function of the pain experience. It consists, according to conditions, in an avoidance reaction or in keeping the painful parts of the body quiet (Hess, 1924), in the first case with the effect that the insult is eased as much as possible and in the second case, as a condition of as favorable restitution as possible. Negative feeling tone, that is to say the affective component, conditions the behavior in other ways too. By associating the pain with the conditions which prevailed at the same time and by remembering them, the subject is able to forestall them. To recognize painful states becomes a motive for avoidance or a defense reaction before the insult. The special efficiency of this connection between subjective experiences of a nociceptive insult and the proper reaction against it is of importance because here the content of consciousness as a motive of behavior can be clearly recognized. To determine the responsible cerebral structures one can adduce experiments on animals in which we have the possibility of controlling the localization of the stimuli by studying serial sections of brains. As far as the experience goes, one has to rely on indicators which, however, in the form of an avoidance reaction or a phonation which is typical for pain, is quite unequivocal. For our goal it is particularly valuable that we also have experiences of which brain surgeons with psychophysiological interests can give an account. They are frequently asked to get rid of pain by an operation. In order to be sure of their ground, they have to orient themselves by localizing stimulations where they can be helped by the brain anatomist and the patient. The latter can talk about the experience due to stimulation. In the course of such operations, numerous experiences have been collected (Hassler, 1960; Hassler and Riechert, 1959). From a brief report, we can take the following: if during a stereotactic operation for pain the small-celled nucleus in which the tractus spinothalamicus ends in the thalamus, the nucleus ventralis caudalis parvocellularis is stimulated with a bipolar electrode with a distance between the electrodes of 2 to 5 mm., it regularly produces an outcry, with painful expression in the face, when middle frequencies are used, that is to say, 25 to 50 per second; at times a tetanic contraction of the contralateral arm is produced and a strong feeling of pain which has its maximum in circumscribed parts of the skin of the opposite side of the body. The quality of the pain experienced is given as cramping, piercing, tearing, burning, or cold pain. By shifting the electrode medially, the pain experiences as well as the other signs can be elicited in the neighboring higher segments of the body. If, on the basis of these localized findings, one proceeds to destroy stereotactically by coagulation the parvocellular nucleus which lies posteriorly and ventrally to the main sensory nucleus, electrical excitations of the same kind become ineffective so that no sensations are elicited.

If one tries to evaluate the experiences which have just been related for the task which we have given us, there can be no doubt about the connections between a content of consciousness which can be defined qualitatively and the excitation of a certain cerebral organ and therefore also about the organic motivation of a certain behavior. This unequivocal connection between structure, organ and subjective experience is, however, not to be interpreted as a causal connection which can be psysiologically investigated. The question is really on another plane. In particular, the findings leave it open whether the subjective experience is an effect of the artificial stimulation at this place or whether we have a projection of the excitatory processes into a reticular formation of elements whose response is correlated with a specific sensory content of consciousness. When one looks around for reasons which speak for the one or the other variant, it should be kept in mind that we can suppress voluntarily to some extent the reaction to pain but not pain itself, which speaks for a distinction between the place where the experience occurs and where the behavior motivated by it originates. In the same way, we have to interpret the anticipated reaction which we discussed previously, where we involuntarily react to a painful sensation even before the threatening insult has occurred. To make these findings and the consequences which flow from them more precise, we have to mention that from other parts than the nuclei which we named above, we never elicited a pain sensation by electrical stimulation, in spite of a great number of operations. Another possibility, that the stimulation of the thalamic structures which are in closest connection with the pain experience are projected in a modified form to the higher planes of the cerebral cortex, cannot be answered unequivocally. This much is certain, that in man there is no cortical area from which a pain sensation can be elicited. This is based on a large number of observations (Penfield and Rasmussen, 1950).

Another experience has to do with the ablation of parts of the cortex. If in such operations the so-called adversive eye field in the occipital lobe is ablated, no nociceptive stimuli on the side opposite to the lesion are heeded. For the typical pain experiences, evidently extirpations of the adversive eye field in the frontal lobe are also of importance (Hassler, 1960), because after such an operation nociceptive stimuli are no longer noticed. An analogous insufficiency is also found for other sensory qualities.

The position of the post-central convolution in the organization of the pain system needs a detailed investigation.

While the stimulation experiments give no positive answer, the excision of parts of the post-central convolution leads for a long time to a definite contralateral hypalgesia (Hassler, 1960).

If we now pass on to observations which concern the derivations of electrical potentials in connection with the experience of pain, we must mention first of all that in chronic states of pain the cortex which can be seen from the outside shows no electrophysiological signs. However, in animal experiments we can make observations which belong in this context. This concerns the rhythmic electrical activity in the region of phylogenetically old parts of the brain, the allocortex. This is a symptom of peripheral painful stimuli in the rabbit and the cat (MacLean and Delgado, 1953). These changes in the electrical activity, particularly in the cornu ammonis, are connected with emotional processes which go hand in hand with the waking reaction in the phylogenetically younger isocortex and result in a flattening of the EEG, which, however, also occurs after other stimuli which have an affective tone. In any case, a comparatively high stimulus intensity has to be exceeded, so that we have to think about the possibility that consciousness of pain is the extreme case of a general reaction concerning needs (Rein, 1939). We have to repeat that analogous relations are also met with when stimuli in other sensory systems come into consciousness, as in the sector of the equilibratory proprioceptivity. Stimuli of small intensity are worked over unconsciously, while stronger stimuli lead to changes of consciousness which then motivate a goal-directed behavior. Seen from this angle, the contents of consciousness give the last remaining security for protective reactions which are usually automatically regulated.

After we have learned about the relations which obtain in a primitive sensory quality, that is to say, in pain and also in the experience of deviations from the stabilized posture, differences between the sensory effects of various qualities become clearest when we go to a system which is highly organized. For men as well as the most diverse vertebrates, we have in the first line to think about visual experiences which have been examined in great detail as far as correlations between neuronal happenings and subjective experiences are concerned. Added to this is the fact that the morphological and functional relations of the visual system are particularly suited for comparative psychophysiological analysis; moreover, there are direct connections with the direction of the gaze which have been discussed in the previous chapter.

In the spirit of comparative psychophysiology, we go once more first to predatory fish as a test subject. As we said, in decisive situations its behavior is governed by the eye. This applies to the attack of an object of prey as well as fleeing into a hiding place. Here the important question is whether this fish is governed purely by a reflex mechanism, or whether an even quite narrow perception gives the impulse. In observations directed to this point, nothing could be elicited that allowed even a tentative judgment. We cannot answer this question.

In birds one can, with advantage, use the concrete example of the parrot which has been well observed both from an ecological point of view and after brain operations (Kalischer, 1905). We have here indications of an ability to integrate some point-by-point sensations to form figures, and, furthermore, to fix these as memory traces. The one as well as the other is shown by the bird through his reactions to certain visual impressions. By connecting momentary with former experiences and by arranging his behavior accordingly, he shows not only that he recognizes relevant objects and processes, but also that he realizes their importance for himself. Particularly convincing are anticipatory reactions when he sees something to which he reacts on the basis of former experience in a prehensive or protective manner, as in turning away or by a preventive attack or by fleeing from it. The interpretation of such behavior as an expression of visual experience and evaluation is corroborated by his "holding back" when confronted with unknown objects, for instance, with fruits which he has never seen. Also, when he meets people whose acquaintance he has not made yet and from whom therefore he does not know what to expect, he shows definite caution. As far as the co-ordination of visually integrative accomplishments is concerned, we think of the motor reactions which are steered by the tectum opticum, a formation of the midbrain, according to the position of the stimulus object in the visual field. We have to assume, therefore, that these are connected with visual experiences and that from there the visual forms and processes activate those motor stimuli patterns whose eccentric projection becomes expressed as a goal-directed pattern of a movement.

Going over to the cat, a highly organized mammal, we again turn our attention to the goal-directed reaction of the gaze and the consequent prehensive and productive behavior, with the idea of learning about the pertinent cerebral organizations. In this connection there comes to mind a small paper which was published many years ago ("Vom Lichtreiz zur bildhaften Wahrnehmung," Hess, 1952b). In the meantime it has become clear, however, that the problem cannot be attacked from the periphery, but rather must be approached from the ability and active tendency to create contents of consciousness. This is part of a genuine drive to see in consciousness a specific potency bound to life by concrete sensations which are integrated to perceptions.

In the case of the visual system, all parts are designed so that by specifically organized elements the appropriate stimuli are brought about, differentiated according to qualities, quantities, and directional signs. Following the centripetal stimuli, a stepwise integration comes about that organizes the multiplicity of signals to figures or to spatial forms which are furthermore labeled by frequency equivalents. Thus prepared, the conditions for receiving these ordered processes in consciousness are fulfilled. That we do not realize ourselves this transposition from the objective into the subjective does not change the fact of definite connections, because our ability to understand is no criterion for actual connections.

Coming back to the visual perception of the cat, it is of interest whether a goal-directed gaze has anything to do with sensations related to the tectal apparatus or whether it is simply a reflex mechanism. In unexpected optic events which are pictured in the peripheral part of the retina, the latter is the more likely. In differentiated processes, however, which are projected into the eye from one side, a perception connected with the tectum opticum cannot be excluded, at least not as a modest part in connection with higher cerebral processes, which as a second and third instance have to be looked for in the occipital lobe of the brain. As we have to deduce from this gaze reaction, we have to take into account other parts of the visual system. Part of these are probably structures which, as mentioned, are situated in the diencephalon (p. 80). Their contribution becomes manifest after a one-sided lesion is made in the region of the diencephalon, but with visual tracts left completely intact. Some cats behave as though they were blind on the side opposite the coagulation by diathermy and completely blind after coagulation on both sides (Hess, 1943b). The experimental animals, when they walk around, bump without hesitation into a barrier which is in their way. Also, they do not stop when they come to the end of the operating table; they go into the void with one leg and fall over the edge. They pay no attention to the feeding trough that is on the table, but step into it if it happens to be in their way. The visual insufficiency after one-sided coagulation in the diencephalon is also shown by the fact that the cat consistently walks only to the side of the coagulation focus [3] and goes after a piece of meat only if it is given on that side of the visual field to which it walks freely and certainly. As surely as the sensations are gone in the way which has been described and as the visual deficit is connected with destruction in the region of the diencephalon, it has so far not been possible for us to give a more detailed explanation.

A better understood member of the cerebral organization located in the diencephalon is the alternate projection of the retinal elements of the right and left eye in the lateral geniculate body (Minkowski, 1913). The stimuli conducted to one or the other side are for optical reasons similar but not quite identical. They fuse at a higher level and the parallactic shifts of the two pictures are, as is well known, used as a criterion for the third dimension. In this whole situation, the question arises whether this depth experience is the result of an integration in the lateral geniculate body. According to Minkowski, the fusion does not come about in these cerebral formations. The right and left systems are alternately located in the shape of thin layers in the geniculate body, but they are still separated by myelinated lamellae. In all likelihood, according to Minkowski, only the first step for fusion is being taken here, while the complete fusion happens at the next higher projection, namely in the visual cortex. It is possible that the integral fusion of a spatial experience does not always happen in the same way but depends on circumstances, for instance, on the intensity of stimulation, and perhaps also on the size of the excited regions and of the fine structure of the stimulated pattern. Thus the law would be fulfilled that a complete organization only occurs in steps. We have to expect,

[3] TRANSLATOR'S NOTE.—This has been corrected from the German sentence following a correspondence with Dr. K. Akert, who got in touch with Professor Hess himself. I wish to thank both of them once more for their co-operation.

moreover, that the very interesting psychophysiological phenomenon of fusion will be investigated by modern methods. We have to take into account that the accommodations of the lens and the convergence movements of the eye are also used to determine depth of space.

Since this lamellar arrangement of the ascending fibers from right and left eye had been discovered and the consequences had been discussed, further research was carried out by registering the electrical activity of single neurons in the visual cortex while only one point was stimulated in the retina (Hubel and Wiesel, 1961). To clarify completely the correspondence between functional and morphological organization and the ensuing integration of the neuronal correlates of depth vision, further researches are necessary, for which, however, we probably will not have to wait very long.

The next step showing the order of the visual system leads to experiences after extirpation of one or both occipital lobes. As everybody knows, in the higher vertebrates and man it is here that the large mass of fibers from the eye end, after having been sorted out as to right and left fibers in the lateral geniculate body. Since there are far-reaching correspondences between the relations which are valid for man and for higher visually organized animals, it will be simplest for the exposition as well as for the understanding if we summarize the findings for all forms. We will first of all put in the foreground the subjective symptoms in stimulation and extirpation of the visual area of man, because from man we can get information by language. Occasionally, suitable undertakings are indicated, as we said, either for diagnostic or therapeutic reasons, which make the brain surgeon ask active co-operation of the patient. As far as the results are concerned, we will first of all pay attention to the effects which can be obtained from the cortex of the occipital lobe (Penfield and Rasmussen, 1950). In immediate connection with electrical stimulation a patient reported that he saw red or green; in another case, yellow or blue. It frequently happened that the light was seen to move slowly even when the stimulating electrode did not change position. These subjective manifestations of the artificially induced stimulus of cortical elements could be repeated. Such a finding has the value of an unequivocal sign for correlating a specific content of consciousness to definite cerebral substrates. The authors also report on cases where simple forms such as colored stars or wheels, colored disks, or colored balls were seen. Such visual experiences, whose connotations related to former experiences, could not, however, be reproduced because after the first stimulus only a simple experience of light became manifest. The recognition of Gestalten is extinguished more easily than elementary experiences.

If we move the stimulus to a neighboring region in the same person, the visual experience changes, in such a way that she now sees white marks in that part of the visual field which is opposite the locus of the stimulus. At the same time, a red point could appear on the stimulated side. In this way, relations between areas are documented into which both halves of the visual field are projected. The functional effect is probably the reciprocal influence of opposing parts of the visual field. The two halves certainly do not work quite independently of each other. Further experiences of Penfield concern stimulations in regions which are situated further forward, that is to say, within the secondary visual cortex. The content of consciousness which was evoked from this region corresponded in some cases also to moving star-like shapes. Other patients saw dancing or flickering lights in white or yellow. Furthermore, after stimulaton of these regions, just as from the primary visual cortex, the patients had the experience of white marks, generally on the opposite side of the visual field. In rarer cases, there were also red points on the stimulated side. What could not be produced by electrical stimulation in either the primary or secondary zone were more complex and meaningful figures. That such contents of consciousness could be elicited by electrical stimulation from other parts of the cortex we will hear later on.

In contrast to the similarity of subjective manifestation of artificially induced stimulation in either the primary or secondary visual cortex, the deficits after extirpation of one or the other cortex are quite different. While there is a hemianopia after one-sided extirpation of the primary visual cortex in the visual fields of both eyes, and while the experience of light is almost completely gone after bilateral extirpation, one does not find such profound deficits after an operation in which only the secondary visual cortex has been ablated. This shows that already the primary visual cortex is in close relation to subjective experiences, perhaps without finer differentiation of the visual experience. The secondary visual cortex would then have the task of developing visual experiences of a higher order from the complexes which were given it by the primary cortex. Relation to formations, whose function is the coining and reactivation of primitive engrams, has been proved for both regions. From both places we activate by electrical stimulation experiences which are identified with pictures which were induced in a normal way on former occasions.

A surprising similarity with the symptoms which are induced by electrical stimulation is the reason to refer briefly here to effects of a chemically defined substance, namely, lysergic acid diethylamide (LSD) (Stoll, 1947). The proband who either by chance or in an auto-experiment has come into oral contact with this substance shows a change in his ability to perceive. Most likely, he sees, when his eyes are closed, green or red fog; yellow stripes; tendencies to primitive movement such as dancing flames; scintillating, spraying, fast or slow flowing; a vortex of sparks; or moving spots. Also, certain shapes which have to be considered as evoked engrams, appear without an external reason, e.g., arches, rings, colored circles, ellipses, etc. Even more complex patterns can become contents of consciousness, such as fences, nets, spiders, ornaments, and other figures which obviously are connected with visual impressions from former physiological experiences. In this group are included visual experiences such as seeing of snowflakes, leaves and ferns, woodwork, etc. Finally, the process may assume forms which are correlated with quite definite optical experiences and are connected with intellectually experienced pictures. Here we should mention the seeing of chromosomes and technical structures such as the wheel of a turbine, also the manifestation of benzol rings in people who are interested in chemistry. The character of the artificial content of consciousness is underlined by the statement in the last case that the picture which came up as a visual experience caused the comment that the chemist would see benzol rings everywhere. It is also remarkable that the contents of consciousness which come up under LSD will not completely take the place of reality in spite of their clearness. Actual experiences may come at least partly to consciousness, which is also the case in electrical stimulation of the visual sphere.

In judging the fusion of unreal imagination-like illusions with actual experiences and reactivated parts of former experiences, one has to keep in mind that such errors are not without psychophysiological parallels. We can, for instance, go over obstacles of all kinds in the woods without a mishap, even when at the same time we think about things which are connected with visual experiences of quite a different order. Such a mixing of different contents of consciousness normally has its limits, namely, where the attention is definitely occupied by exteroceptive stimuli. Then those contents of consciousness which are not supported by direct experiences are suppressed, in which case the importance of the development of the consecutive contents of consciousness shows the way.

Characteristic for visual experience as they appear under LSD is the inclination to repetition. Certain figures are seen in the plural at the same time or they reappear again and again after having faded away. A special case is a micropsia or macropsia which occasionally appears, in other words, a mistake about the actual size of seen objects. Photoptic experiments show us that the correct interpretation of size is based on the relation of perceived distance to the size of the picture on the retina. Under LSD, the computation of these two quantities can be disturbed, in certain cases by deformation of the criteria which are interpreted when we perceive distance. What we have in mind is a shift of the intensity of the impulses when we accommodate to a clear picture and when we converge the two eyes to make two monocular pictures congruent. Obviously, the dosage of the impulses is not commensurate with the optical situation under LSD. This is an interpretation, as we will hear later, which is also valid for goal-directed motor impulses (pp. 120, 121).

Another variant of disturbed organization of visual impressions to a complete picture is given when a pit-like discontinuity in a landscape is seen as a hill, when the boundary between meadow and plowed field is seen as a river, or when a wall is seen as a railway embankment. In the last case, wrong performance is still further accentuated by including without any concrete reason electric trolley lines, showing a tendency of the consciousness to seek confirmation from former experiences. In all likelihood, this happens in such a way that these experiences exert a facilitating function in the development of integrated contents of consciousness and can do that all the more readily the lower the thresholds are. Thus it can be understood that traces of cleaning on a glass plate are seen as a fish and colored spots as glittering butterfles or multicolored salamanders. In all of these cases, the desire to see former patterns is expressed.

Remarkable also is the experience that under LSD purely subjective motives, like some experiences which are brought about by electrical stimulation, can evoke feeling tones, in such a manner that one colored pattern is evaluated as agreeable and another colored tone as disagreeable.

If one compares the visual experience evoked on the one side by electric stimulation and on the other side by the chemical agent, it stands to reason to assume a heightened excitability under the influence of LSD of the elements which are aggregated to cerebral formations. Because the thresholds are lower, some of the fine physiological oscillations of the state of excitation work as true excitations for the formulation of contents of consciousness.

If one tries to draw any consequences which point to further progress from the correspondence between the symptoms after LSD and the results of localized electrical stimulation, one realizes the great heuristic value of a comparative analysis of the effects of different influences on cerebral function.

Important progress in finding correlations between neuronal processes and visual contents of consciousness has been achieved by recording action potentials from single cells of the cortex in a well worked-out program (Jung, 1960, 1961; Jung, Creutzfeldt, and Baumgartner, 1952). Out of the rich experimental findings, we select the following: for light-dark seeing we find a very good quantitative correlation between cortical neuronal activity in the cat and psychophysiological observations in man. Thus if we change the intensity of light, the objective signs, namely, the changes in frequency of neuronal activity, correspond to subjective signs: the experienced brightness. Furthermore, it has been found that neuronal elements of the cortex react reciprocally to optic stimulation of the retina; some react positively with increased frequency and others negatively with decreased or completely lacking discharges. According to R. Jung, a neuronal equilibrium is thus

103

insured and simultaneous discharge of all neurons is avoided. This ordered neuronal pattern is very similar to the reciprocal organization of the vegetativum which we have found previously. It proves, just as these do, a positive effect of suppressor action. Facilitation and suppression of neurons which work reciprocally are found in the same field, and suppression of synergistic neurons in adjacent regions. In the case of the visual function, the subjective correlate is a specific experience of light or dark in certain parts of the visual field and the reciprocal action of retinal places which was postulated by Hering. Other results have to do with the (relative) correlation between the frequency of objectively shown neuronal discharges in flicker on the one side and subjective fusion of these impulses on the other side, and this correlation between maximum neuronal discharges in flicker of middle frequency and the strongest subjective brightness of just this flicker frequency (effect of Brücke). It was further found that in simple diffused light, there is a reciprocal suppression between antagonistic neurons, i.e., a competition which is again analogous to the functional organization of the vegetative nervous system. Added to this, there is a collateral suppression of synergistic neurons in contrasting optic stimuli, thus making subjectively clear the structure of a picture, as in paintings of advertisements. The latter relations correspond to the simultaneous contrast (cf. Jung, 1961). If one presents to the experimental animal, the cat, contrasting stimuli (light-dark stripes) and leads off with a micro-electrode from single fibers of the optic nerve or from neurons of the lateral geniculate body or the cortex (Area 17), it can then be shown that the single fibers of the optic nerve and correspondingly the later neurons register the light which falls on a comparatively large surface of the retina. The light of this receptive field is integrated in such a way that simultaneous contrast as well as sudden changes in the intensity of light become accentuated, and in darkness periodic after-discharges occur which are correlated with the successive contrast. The activation of the neurons in stimuli of simultaneous contrast corresponds to the subjective impression in the sensory physiological experiments in which, as is well known, the impression of greatest brightness is registered at the boundary between the white and black field and the most intense black is experienced in a bright surrounding. At the same amount of light, the maximum objective stimulation of the light-activated neurons appears at the boundary between light and dark and those of the dark-activated neurons at the dark-light boundary. The reaction of the fibers of the optic nerve, of the neurons of the lateral geniculate body and of the visual cortex shows principally the same behavior. Finally, correlations between the cortical electrical effect from afferent stimuli from the brain stem (intralaminar thalamus) and subjective experience were found, as well as other influences which manifest themselves both in the objective neuronal happenings and in the subjective experience.

If we now turn our attention to the auditory system and investigate its work as far as the correlation between the contents of consciousness and the functional organization of the brain is concerned, we take our departure again from experiences in diagnostic investigations of neurological patients (Penfield, 1955). It should be mentioned in the first place that we can have a primitive experience like chirping in electrical stimulation of the temporal lobe. Elementary also is the hearing of a rustle which was likened by the patient to the auditory experience "when the wind rustles through the trees." In another case, the electrical stimulation in the region of the temporal lobe gave, according to Penfield, an experience like ringing of bells or like playing of the organ. In the latter case, the stimulus was localized in the upper right margin of the temporal lobe. The auditory experience given by the stimulus was further made precise by the patient when he said that the song he heard was known to him. The auditory experience after electrical stimulation of the temporal cortex was still more highly evaluated when a mother heard one of her children and recognized by the tone of voice which one of her children talked. Similarly complex is the auditory experience in which the electrical stimulation was correlated with the content of consciousness in which boys called out. The patient added that the experience which was thus artificially reproduced had actually happened years ago. How a circumscript electrical stimulation can develop a highly organized pattern, a structured auditory experience, is shown by the example in which the patient heard how his mother telephoned to his aunt to invite her. Here is a reproduction of a whole situation characterized by auditory information.

If we summarize these various experiences regarding the auditory system, it is confirmed that an unspecific stimulus is connected with certain contents of consciousness. If we probe more closely, we see further that these become manifest, according to conditions, in a different manner, sometimes primitively organized, in other cases correlated with a complicated and elaborately worked-out pattern of exitation. Sometimes, as in flashbacks, elements of that layer are included in which engrams are physiologically inscribed.

The prospects of making such representative patterns objectively recognizable as neuronal processes are at the moment not very great. However, the correlation of the cortical artificial stimulation and subjective experience remains, as we already said, a fact. This is also true for the inclusion of reminiscences, which we will discuss more closely under the heading of memory. It has frequently been shown that in certain parts of the temporal lobe, on repeated stimulation at one and the same place, the same content of consciousness is evoked. It can also reappear in a modified form, e.g., at the first stimulation a melody was heard which somebody played on the piano. At repeated stimulations, a singing voice was heard and at another time the same song reappeared, now more clearly recognized as a song from a radio program. All of these electrical stimulations are, according to the published accounts, uniform in the sense that the correlative experience was music or a musical show (except in the case of one single test stimulus). The music had from case to case a slightly different character but the "pattern" was experienced with increasing precision.

Such variations can be understood by assuming that the circumscribed stimulation is somewhat differently propagated from stimulus to stimulus because the response of the elements which are in the neighborhood of the focus changes, either because the threshold varies spontaneously or because the after-effects of a previous activity are still present.

When we discussed the visual system, we called attention to the fact that under the influence of a structurally defined substance (LSD) contents of consciousness come about similar to those evoked after electrical stimulation of the visual spheres. A correlation between the two modes of artificial stimulation was seen in the fact that elements ordered on a microscopic level were put into a heightened excitability by LSD. This is confirmed by the experiences made in the auditory system. Because the patient who has been given LSD is supersensitive to acoustic stimuli, the touching of type on the typewriter is heard so loud that the clatter is a disagreeable, even unbearable noise (Stoll, 1947). This shows also that under certain circumstances the auditory as well as the visual experience has an affective component whose activation according to the experience discussed previously must be due to an influence on a lower level which must be in the brainstem. We should also note that the elements of the auditory system are less influenced by these psychotropic substances, because without external stimuli there is less tendency to heightened activity which would show up in a spontaneous auditive content of consciousness.

In connection with the accounts of subjective manifestations of cortical stimulation, we will now report on the consequences of ablation of certain cortical regions for the function of the auditory system. We know that cats in whom the auditory region of the endbrain has been removed lose first of all the learned ability to differentiate between tones of various pitch (Meyer and Woolsey, 1952). However, these animals are able to relearn this feat, and relearning does not take any more time than learning with an intact brain (Neff and Diamond, 1958). From the functional defect after ablation of a cortical area one concludes that the learned ability to differentiate is bound to cerebral structures. Thus the relearning must be due to a vicarious effect of a functionally equivalent organization, in the sense of a complete compensation, probably by a neighboring part of the brain, as this has been shown for the remembering of a movement (Cole and Glees, 1954). However, it does not seem to be quite so simple, since even after extirpation of all known auditory areas of the cortex, cats can still remember to differentiate between tones of various pitches (Butler, Diamond, and Neff, 1957). Such experiences show that even in the plane of the mesencephalic projections, the effects can be covered up by compensatory effects, perhaps not differentiated ones. This is corroborated in some ways by the effects of attempts to train cats from whom the whole cortex had been removed. It was shown that such animals are able to hear pitches and intensities just as well as normal cats. They are, however, unable to identify specific structures of tones (Rose and Woolsey, 1958). We still have to wait for further clarification of the correlation between subjective manifestation of the auditory system and the underlying cerebral organization.

In one direction, a deeper insight has been achieved by deriving action potentials, namely, in connection with stimulation of certain points in the cochlea in the inner ear of cats and monkeys. It was shown that between the cortex and the cochlea there is a point-to-point correspondence. This means that there is a precisely ordered transmission of impulses by the receptors to the auditory sector of the temporal lobe. Remarkably, this same order is repeated in the secondary zone but going in the opposite direction (Woolsey and Walzl, 1942). Concerning the correlation between objective and subjective order, one could show in the dog by evoked potentials that differences in frequency of octaves are represented by the same distances of cortical foci (Tunturi, 1950).

Considering these findings, it is odd that, in a prolonged acoustic stimulation at the same pitch, the electrical activity wanders along the band of projection. As a possible explanation, we consider that the excitability of elements which responded first gradually decreases and neighboring elements now respond which primarily were less susceptible and were also inhibited by the excitation of the first elements. Here, too, we can go back to experiences from the motor zone (p. 82). Subjectively, such reserves are instances of constant perception, if the stimulus intensity is kept constant.

Another problem concerning the auditive system and the relation between contents of consciousness and cerebral organization flows from the fact that one is able to point with a fair degree of certainty to the direction from which noise comes to our ears. In optic stimuli, the relations are simpler, insofar as excitation of the light receptors is correlated with the direction from wihch the ray of light comes. Added to this are messages from the oculomotor apparatus which arise when the eyes are moved according to the sensation of direction, whether directly by the movement or indirectly by the tensions produced when the movements have been executed. In the ear the local sign is missing, or rather it is used for differentiation of pitch. Therefore, we need other criteria that can function as an indication of direction. During the last few years, further insight has been gained into this problem. Partly, experiences were used which were made in connection with the technical development of transmission and working over of electro-acoustic information (Keidel, Wigand, and Keidel, 1960a). The difference in time between the acoustic impressions on the ear which was towards the source of the noise, and was therefore hit first by the impulses, and the slightly later stimulation of the ear which was away from the source of the noise was found to be an important factor. A second factor that gives information about directions is the difference in the intensity of the acoustic stimuli that are taken up by one ear or the other, again depending on the position of the ears relative to the source of noise. Based on observations in animals, the neural apparatus, which on the basis of temporal differences innervates those muscles which lead to a turning of the head to the source of noise, is to be put closer to the periphery. Apart from this, the many functions of the ear show, according to Keidel (1960b), that these must be due to complex structures and that only a statistical working over of the signals that come from the ears to higher levels can be considered. This interpretation is corroborated by the fact, among others, that there are ascending as well as descending connections for the stimulation complexes, which in their turn influence the peripheral neuronal dispositions. Summing up all these experiences there is shown again the close working together of the cortex and the subcortex. Furthermore, both of the two possible criteria, i.e., the difference in the time and the difference in intensity, are used in binaural hearing to determine the direction of the noise and thus give vital information to consciousness.

As far as the organization of neuronal dispositions and their relation to function in the auditory experience goes, one knows today that the intensity of the noise is reproduced not only by the greater number of discharges but also, as one had to expect, by the number of fibers involved. To this is added the proof by von Békésy (1952) that when the vibrations of the basilar membrane are transmitted to the cortex, a focusing of the pattern goes hand in hand. It is pointed up to a "maximum" in the distribution of intensity, just as was shown for the cortical central projection of retinal stimulation (Jung, 1958).

If one looks over what has been said so far about the order of neuronal processes and the correlated contents of consciousness, it becomes clear how the stimuli taken up by the sense organs are integrated step by step to patterns and are prepared for assimilation by consciousness. How the transmission of neuronal patterns to contents of consciousness finally takes place is here too hidden from a causal understanding.

After this discussion, first of elementary sensory impressions and then of more highly organized sensory functions, in both cases from the viewpoint of connections between neuronal processes and contents of consciousness, we will briefly mention other sensory systems. We will consider, among others, the control of posture and movements as a function of the equilibratory organs in connection with proprioceptivity. Subjectively, it becomes manifest as an orientation in space in a particular relation to gravity; furthermore, in relation to the translatory or rotatory passive change of posture. The system of proprioceptivity, on the other hand, registers and integrates the tension of the tendons and muscles, as well as the tension in and around the joints, including tension of the overlying skin. The objective adequate stimulus is completely the business of somatic physiology and is clear. Rather new are researches which have to do with the nervous impulses that reach the cortex. There is neither room nor space to go into details. We can only point to the work of S. Andersson and B. E. Gernandt (1954). Our own observations also give some worthwhile hints (Hess, 1954a, 1956). Apart from the publications concerning effects of stimulation and grouping of loci of stimulation, detailed work has been done on cerebral organization (Hassler, 1956a and 1956b).

Summarizing the results of these investigations, one obtains data on the cortical projection of specific systems of the receptors of afferent pathways and interpolated neuron groups that lead the activating impulses to the cortex. Finally, we should discuss the cerebral organization of the olfactory and taste systems. About the former, one can get detailed information from Adey (1959), who reports particularly the important work of Adrian; about the latter, we point to the work of Benjamin and Pfaffmann (1955), Benjamin and Akert (1959), and Landgren (1957).

MEMORY

Several times we mentioned that a perception that comes about by sensory stimulation may bring into consciousness things that were experienced formerly. Generally, it is easy for each person to find that what he was reminded of actually happened at a former time. Similarly, everybody can become convinced by his own experience that the connection between the former contents of consciousness with what happens now is due to similarity, which means that there is a close connection between the present and the past conscious states concerning certain qualities, forms, temporal structures, and causal connections. The parts of the experience that are important may remain accessible for minutes, hours, days, or sometimes even many years.

Apart from a reactivation of external happenings, that is to say of any so-called engrams, spontaneous ideas may have a corresponding effect. The spontaneity may be false, insofar as some member of a prolonged flow of thoughts may lead to a reactivation without our being conscious of it. The opposite of this is the result of a systematic remembering of exteroceptive contents of consciousness which, like the process of learning, are repeated many times in the same sequence and thus fixed, frequently in a long and complicated concatenation, in the memory.

If one tries to find circumstances which are conditions for the presentation of rich contents of consciousness in the memory, we find that multiplicity and differentiation presuppose a large extension of the projection or of the space which is given over to the engrams. This is no different from a fixation of experiences and ideas in writing. If we keep the size of the letters constant, one needs a greater surface for writing the richer the content. This simile is not theory, but it corresponds to a geometric law when we keep track of the size of the signs. As a biological happening, phylogeny shows an impressive example in the increase of brain size with increasing differentiation of the control possibilities that are specific for the species. With the increase of multiplicity of sensory and motor, and also of combinatory, effects, there occurs an increase in mass, particularly of those formations in which the motoric representation is located and also of those to which the stimulation of the receptors of the sensory organs are projected.

Apart from the geometric relations among multiplicity, differentiation, and to a certain extent intensity of cerebral effects, time finally plays a role. One of the reasons for this is the fact that the transmission of excitation takes a certain time that is proportional to the distance between the co-operating formations. Furthermore, the speed of transmission plays a role insofar as speed depends on the cross section of the fibers. Altogether this shows that distance and speed of transmission take space. One may consider the picture given by Penfield and Boldrey (1937) concerning the extent and the arrangement of the elements of sensory and motor quality, and one will find out how much the tongue and face, as well as the

hands, are accentuated according to their functional importance. The relationship which is thus expressed one sees confirmed by the findings of the authors in a functional way,
because in the diencephalon the numerous points of stimulation
are about evenly distributed, but those in the anterior extremity become activated far more often than those in the
posterior one. It cannot be doubted that this finding mirrors
the more multifarious effects and the greater skill of the anterior extremity as compared to the posterior one. Therefore,
for reasons of probability, they are more frequently hit by the
stimulating electrode.

It is now justified to ask what the relation of the projective
field, that is to say between the occupied space and the multiplicity of subcortical and cortical representation areas has to
do with memory. The answer is given by man and animals if
they rapidly recognize a threatening danger and therefore are
able to avoid it quickly and skilfully. In the free-living animal,
a small difference of reaction time and precision of action may
determine life or death. Accordingly, an order is more valuable
in which the patterns given by the memory are as close as
possible to a layer in which the sensations coming from the
sense organs are integrated and are correlated with experience
in the form of a pattern. One can see that contents of consciousness which have the criteria of the past tense may be
elicited by some circumscript electric stimulations (p. 106).
When the impulses from the electrode spread further out,
those elements too are stimulated which in analogy to
local signs of visual and tactile receptors bear a temporal
sign as a content of memory. Thus it can be understood that
an electrically evoked content of consciousness may coincide
with the experience of having gone through this already once
before, the déjà-vu phenomenon (p. 147). The propinquity
between elements which are arranged in patterns that are experienced now and those that represent a similar pattern from

the past is expressed, as we said, by the fact that both are evoked at the same time by a larger stimulus because they are immediately adjacent to each other.

As important as the connections between the spatial extent of functionally specific formations and their effect, are certain results of electrical stimulation, particularly in the temporal lobe. In the first place, we again have to think of the experiences which Penfield made in connection with diagnostic problems in man (1958a). The so-called déjà-vu phenomenon and a possible interpretation has just been discussed. Also, some cases, in which by electrical stimulation of certain circumscript parts of the temporal lobe complex contents of consciousness were evoked and were experienced by the patient as a memory of real happenings, can only be a deception because elements which are normally used for engram patterns are within the ranges of action of electrical stimulation. A precise control of personal experiences verified by other persons could give information and thus could give important clues about the cerebral organization which is at the base of memory. Other relations have to be assumed in those cases in which electrical stimulation is answered by contents of consciousness which comprise information from several senses. Here we have to assume larger connections for the development of complicated patterns of excitation. Occasionally, excitations converge in specific territories in which the various excitations, from primary, secondary, or occasionally even from tertiary projection fields, are integrated. Which parts can be assumed for this function may be mentioned when we talk about extirpation experiments. Here it is still of importance, however, that in working out and reactivating experiences, a subjective evaluation is included and that this may play an active role. Finally, exchanges between language designations of learned and remembered conceptions (Thiele, 1928) which belong to a rather large category show that the working out of experiences occurs in an order which is objectively given. In such a way, it works selectively. We mean by this that the process of en-gramming comes about under the influence of causal con-nections which combine the elements of certain contents of consciousness.

Further experimental experiences which concern the mem-ory have to do with the learning of the ability to differentiate between successive sensory stimulations of similar quality; for instance, between tones of different pitch which are heard one after the other. It has been shown that by circumscript ablations in the region of the auditory sphere the result of such training can be deleted (Meyer and Woolsey, 1952). We can thus conclude that the tone which was given first and which serves as a standard cannot be reactivated. The fact that the lost ability can be relearned by new training has to be related to the use of reserve elements, which become functional if the structures that are supra-ordinated are lost. Such compensatory mechanisms are not restricted to memory; we meet them also in the region of the motor sphere. Here, too, a learned skilful movement can be retrained with success after destruction of the innervating pattern, as was shown by the co-ordinated use of elements which were hierarchically of a lower order. We can conclude, therefore, that in the plane of the mesenceph-alon, representative engrams are fixed and can be reactivated, at least if a suppression from a higher cortical plane is elimini-nated. Corresponding experiences show that the cerebral or-ganization has reserve elements in the brain stem which can on a given occasion take the place of cortical dispositions and, as we explained, can be made subservient to the memory.

When we speak about memory we should also discuss for-getting. The obliteration of experiences is, as is well known, largely dependent on the time that has elapsed since the mem-ory trace was engrammed. In the fixation and the perseverance of engrams, the affective component which goes with the experience plays a decisive role. When in reactivation the mood is often once more brought out in the same way as during engramming, it shows that the neuronal pattern is connected with the representation of affective agitation. This connection remains in the memory. Relativity of memory shows up if one remembers years later something that had happened in all its details as soon as one meets a similar situation. Frequently, however, after longer intervals, details only come up by and by. A certain rank order is expressed on the basis of subjective evaluation, and this rank order, in its turn, is probably correlated with the depth of the engram in the neuronal pattern. Particularly well-remembered elements of the pattern can remain in spite of time and the attacks of new impressions when everything else is gone from the memory. In spite of that, they remain efficient and the latent tension becomes obvious in one way or another, according to individual disposition and external influences. Thus understood, the psychoanalytic explorations are motivated by the biological aspect of mental processes.

Part of the experimental work which concerns relations between memory and cerebral organization belongs to the control by the so-called delayed reaction, combined with ablation of certain parts of the frontal lobe (Harlow and Settlage, 1948; Meyer, Harlow, and Settlage, 1951; Mishkin and Pribram, 1956). These authors used rhesus monkeys as experimental animals. Efficiency before and after ablation of various parts of the cortex has been studied in detail by many observers during the last twenty years. The results of these experiences are discussed in a paper by K. Bättig and H. E. Rosvold (1962). A proper way to proceed is to show the monkey two empty food containers and then to put a tidbit into one of them. Now one prevents the animal from looking further into the closed containers or even from trying to touch or to open one, by placing a barrier in front of them. After the "delay," which may last a few seconds or even more than one minute, one raises the barrier and allows the animal to open one of the containers. A normal animal learns after a larger number of trials to remember into which container the experimenter has put the tidbit. He hardly ever makes a mistake. If, after this trial, one ablates in the experimental animal a comparatively small region of the frontal lobe, it loses this ability. Also, it can never learn it again.

The successful execution of the test of delayed reaction cannot altogether be attributed to memory. One has observed that such animals are able to solve other problems which have to do with memory in a perfectly normal manner. Thus, a macaque with an ablation of the frontal lobe learns, if one gives the tidbit repeatedly in a container which has a special mark, to choose this one correctly after even longer intervals. He is guided correctly by the mark on the basis of former experience. Without such a visual clue, the damaged animal is unable to remember right and left as abstract conceptions. It therefore appears as though the animal with a damaged frontal lobe either is not able to form an abstract engram or is not able to remember an abstract relation. On the other hand, the memory for concrete signals is intact. Further investigations of these undoubtedly interesting findings are necessary for an unequivocal answer, all the more so since these disturbances of memory can also be found after lesions of certain other parts of the brain. We should not forget the possibility that disturbing factors are at play. We particularly should remember that after ablation in the region of the frontal lobe, a general hyperactivity and a change in emotions occurs (French, 1959). Apart from this, the influence on the frontal lobe can be brought in connection with the just-discussed experimental experience that representations of various sensory qualities "converge" in it as a prerequisite of the integration to a complex pattern of excitation. The subjective correlate of this "convergence" of excitations of different origin is the fusion of a multiplicity of criteria in the form of sensations and perceptions. With this interpretation the many neural connections of the frontal lobe are in accord. (Pribram, Chow, and Semmes, 1953; Rose and Woolsey, 1948).

Finally, other observations on the fate of experiences gained during a lifetime should not be overlooked. We think here especially about the physiological process of aging. The defects which gradually appear are not uniform as regards the time of their engrams. Still, what is new is forgotten more easily than older experiences. The neurological correlates which correspond to the latter are therefore more stable. Experiments have been made which make it probable that the mental activity, part of which is the use of former experiences, is connected with the intactness of cellular structures. We have here in mind observations by C. and O. Vogt; according to these authors, the nucleolus in the nucleus of the ganglion cells is particularly well preserved in those people who have, in spite of a great age, exceptional mental abilities (Vogt, 1947). We only can wish to see this correlation beween subjective abilities and peculiarities of intracellular structure confirmed in a large material. Furthermore, we could wish that gerontology in its broadest aspect would be brought to bear on psychophysiology. For the processes of aging give an unlimited number of examples with great variations and might give information about the correlation between mental abilities and cerebral organization.

If one tries to find still other data which concern the relation between memory and cerebral organization, one will think of the well-known amnesia after cerebral shock as an experiment which is brought about by chance. The loss of memory, which may last a short or long time, of the experiences which were acquired just before the shock (so-called retrograde amnesia) can hardly be understood in any other way then that the ability to remember is an expression of an ordered neuronal pattern. According to this interpretation, the connections are so far loosened by the shock that the functional connection of ordered patterns is suspended; that the newest patterns are particularly hit means that the development of resistant order takes a certain time. Such a maturing time reminds one very much of the transitions of colloids from the sol to the gel state. The later state is also characterized by a structurization which becomes firmer with time. In this connection, we should also mention a happening which was observed quite frequently in our own researches on the diencephalon of the cat and perhaps should be understood as a kind of microshock. This concerns an insufficiency of proprioceptivity for a certain time; which was found on the contralateral anterior extremity after placing the electrodes. As a possible explanation, we thought of the loosening of synaptic connectioins by a local edema. It cannot be excluded, on the other hand, that among the sequelae of a brain shock we have to do with the protective suppression of particularly exposed elements. It is a fact that quiescence by suppression, which favors restitution, is a general biological principle which among others is found where the central innervation of the somatic motor apparatus has been insulted, and also where by stimulation in a certain area of the lateral hypothalamus the normal tonus of the whole musculature of the body is reversibly suppressed, or even completely abolished (Hess, 1954a).

SENSO-MEMO-MOTORIC BEHAVIOR:
INTELLIGENT BEHAVIOR AND LANGUAGE

In the first part we discussed and analyzed examples of behavior typical for the species. Here we briefly come back to a very simple example from my own experience which allows us easily to recognize the motives of reaction. In the orchard, the care of which relaxes me, I see a peach whose color mobilizes a latent drive. The first effect is that visual sensation activates a behavior which complements the aspect which is given from a distance. By reaching out, I bring the fruit within the grasp of my hand, so that by fingering it I become better informed as to how ripe it is. Added to this is the smell, which corroborates the findings of my touch. Thus, visual, tactile, and olfactory sensations bring about an integral experience which places me under the effect of former, now reactivated, contents of consciousness and make me pluck the peach. By eating the fruit of which I have taken possession, taste is added to the experience which, together with the touch sensations that come from the mouth, lead to swallowing after a climax which now releases the tension that led to this action. The active role of memory for the taste that is heightened to greediness should be signified by talking about senso-memo-motor behavior as a motive for my behavior. In point of fact, such experiences are very powerful both in man and in higher vertebrates. For in no other way is the behavior instigated and governed in these forms, e.g., in the cat that smells the rat. The positive feeling tone creates a goal, namely, to go to the source of the smell and, if possible, to obtain a desired piece. Under certain circumstances auditory, in other cases visual, sensations may enhance or hinder the act. The latter happens, for instance, when a cat in sniffing at an object is informed by his temperature sense that the object of his desire is too hot. Thus, even on the basis of elementary sensory functions on a lower level of cerebral organization it comes to a competition that regulates the uptake of food in the long run according to the need and immediately according to the taste.

More complicated situations are present if a desired object moves in an erratic manner. In catching it, the motor innervation is partitioned into a number of actions, the execution of which are way-stations to the goal. The appropriate innervation is guided (as is the whole movement) by the idea of the goal-directed movements, while concomitantly the effect of co-ordinated forces gives the starting position of the next combination of forces.

After this partly repeated and dynamically conceived representation of prehensile behavior, the question of correlation between voluntary innervation and cerebral organization has to be discussed. In the introduction to the experimental part (pp. 38 ff.), we pointed out ways and means which could be used for such investigations. When the experimenter pursues a goal, he has in his mind a disposition concerning the arrangement of the experiment, the realization of which will probably lead to the answer he seeks. An important factor here is the measurement of the spatial and temporal parameters, the results of which are included in the picture and its realization. Since Exner recognized as a guiding principle the control of tensions in joints and tendons and thereby the control of movements, a regulatory picture has been constructed which, ordered by phases, makes this work understandable (Hess, 1941; von Holst, 1955). How contents of consciousness are included in these pictures we will show in some concrete examples. One of these concerns the phenomenon of constancy of space. By this we understand that the environment stands still when we move the eyes, a subjective phenomenon which presupposes a neuronal organization and compensates for the moved eye in which the pictures wander over the retina. According to the scheme given by von Holst, the correction is mediated by a neural feedback system of the motor movements by so-called re-afferents which are stimulated by the movement of the eyes. On this basis, the size constancy of objects seen at different distances can be explained. As mentioned, the retinal image of an object of a given size varies with the distance from the eyes. It is larger when nearer and smaller when farther away. But as a man goes away from us, his size remains unchanged in our experience. In this case, the reduction from the pictured to the experienced size comes about by a "computation" from accommodation, probably with the help of convergence innervation and of peripheral tensions which appear when the convergence is executed again in the sense of a feedback. With the same effect, according to experimentally found facts, the optical distance in a frontal plane is used when the point of fixation is nearer or farther from the eye in the visual space. However, the neuronal patterns which correspond to the theoretically reduced schemata have not yet been discovered. We report on them here all the same because of the heuristic value of exactly thought-out mental experiments, which have their due place as a guide to goal-directed research in physiology just as they have it in theoretical physics and in chemistry where symbols are used. The more complex the relations the more one has to use such work if one wants to experiment according to a plan and not leave too much to blind chance.

A culmination is reached by the sensor-memo-motor behavior and its underlying cerebral organization in articulated language. Above we discussed the development of these psychophysiological accomplishments (pp. 21–23). To repeat briefly what was said there, we keep in mind that man is able to make objective his contents of consciousness in the shape of auditory patterns. The hearer in his turn is guided by his acquired language and is able to transform the acoustic pattern received by his ear into the appropriate contents of his consciousness. The objective aspect of language formulations can be shown electrographically, as many documents show (Gemelli and Pastori, 1935; Gemelli, Sacerdote, and Bellussi, 1955). As far as the cerebral organization is concerned, which is responsible for forming words and sentences, one has tried to localize it by electrical stimulation of the cortex (Penfield and Roberts, 1959). All tests, however, were negative. What could be achieved by these authors phonetically is limited to primitive phonation.

In respect to the frequently astonishing ability of parrots, who have a much simpler brain, to speak, there was a well-motivated although relatively early undertaking to get some hint about their important cerebral organization by stimulation and ablation (Kalischer, 1905), but here too it was never possible to elicit one of the learned words, which under normal conditions were frequently spoken either after the teacher or spontaneously, even those which were used correctly in a given situation. The best that was elicited from the parrot was an unco-ordinated phonation. Certain results led Kalischer to suspect that the frontal brain had something to do with speaking. As it appears to us, this assumption is highly questionable. It is of interest when we think about the relations in men which still have to be discussed that parrots can imitate words if one hemisphere of the forebrain has been ablated. If, however, the other hemisphere is also ablated, the ability to speak is completely lost. On the other hand, parrots with one hemisphere are able to learn new words within a short time. Furthermore, training has shown that motor ability and understanding of words are presented separately, just as in man.

Penfield was somewhat impressed by the fact that, in man, from certain parts of the cortex the flow of spontaneous speaking, for instance of counting, could be interrupted by electrical stimulation (Penfield and Roberts, 1959). In this speech arrest, Penfield found that the structures which were hit are somehow connected with the motor aspect of the language. If, however, one keeps in mind under how many different conditions an impediment of speaking can be brought about, it becomes doubtful whether his conclusion is correct. In point of fact, stronger stimuli break up all order in cerebral processes, whether it is a train of thought, a reactivation of memory, or the flow of a complicated psychomotor process.

More important than stimulation experiments are the chance experiments of nature as a physiologist might call them, namely, the diseases which lead to aphasia. If we correlate such disturbances with cerebral organization, we can base ourselves to some slight extent on our own observations, but we also have to consider the experience of clinicians and of brain specialists in pathological anatomy, e.g., Bay (1952) and Brain (1955); also the comprehensive works of Nielsen (1946), Thiele (1928), Goldstein (1948), and Critchley (1953).

As is well known, comparison of clinical defects with organic defects of the brain have shown that there are close connections between the ability to speak and certain circumscribed parts of the brain which have to be considered as a motor language or better as a speaking center. Somewhat later but still during the classic time of brain research, one heard of experiments which concern connections between understanding of language and a cortical region close to the speaking center, the so-called sensory language center. One is also in general oriented about the peculiarity that the cerebral organization which must be intact if one wants to talk and understand spoken messages is only found in one hemisphere. The neuronal processes that correlate the formulation of acoustic symbols or contents of consciousness with the received acoustic patterns are found on one side of the brain, in right-handed persons on the left side, just like the cortical motor representation in the precentral convolution. In all probability, this one-sided arrangement is due to the fact that the sometimes very complicated patterns for words and their large number which man develops and can transpose to contents of consciousness when he hears them, can work without disturbance and much faster when the neuronal patterns are all in one hemisphere than when the neuronal patterns are on either side and therefore comparatively far apart from each other and have to be correlated by transverse connections. These thoughts, which take into account the functional economy of biological patterns, also apply to the cerebral organization, which is responsible for the skilful and fast manual operation of one hand only.

Another problem concerning the motor side of language is up for discussion when one tries to look into the internal structure of the cerebral organ which is in relation to the various effectors of the apparatus of speech, that is to say, to the muscles of the larynx, the palate, the tongue, and the lips, whose co-ordinated activity brings to phonetic expression the central patterns. That in these central patterns under certain circumstances the mimetic musculature can be included, also the muscles of the arms and hands, and even of the whole body, gives us further information about the structure and function of such a pattern. When the supplementary apparatus brings to expression accents and moods, then it is shown that the contents of consciousness which are correlated with the organization of patterns for sentences and words are evaluated and included in the communication. A contribution to the organization of the speech center is furthermore given by the experience that even in severe defects remnants of language generally remain, e.g., forms of greeting, interjections, yes or no, etc. In people who are used to that sort of thing, swear words may also remain. The unusual resistance of the patterns of innervation to disturbances of the cerebral organization can be due to a particularly deep impregnation, and this may be due, just as in memory, to an affective component of the acoustic symbol. Frequent use of patterns which lead to motor innervations not only makes the structural development of the pattern easier but also makes it more permanent, just as we see in other organs as a consequence of increased use.

Another question concerns the co-ordination of an affective experience with the contents of consciousness, if these are given linguistic expression or if they are taken up by ear. The experience that affects irradiate into the vegetativum speaks for the notion that they are anchored at lower levels in which there is an intimate contact with the central organization of vegetative functions, that is to say, in the region of the brain stem which therefore very likely contributes to the dynamics of verbal expression.

Thus we are able to understand a psychophysiologically very interesting variation of motor aphasia in which words or even sentences can be reproduced but in which no accents are present nor a rhythm which enlivens the speaking. Normally, such a variation in speaking or in spoken expression shows an evaluation of the contents of consciousness that the speaker wants to transmit. By accents we want to show which parts of the sentence have a feeling tone. Rhythm gives to the speech a well-rounded form and makes it easier for the partner in the conversation to listen. On the other hand, good as well as bad tones signify subjective manifestations of feeling which try to gain expression by mimetic gestures and by the tone of language and which are associated with the formulation of words and sentences. If the neuronal correlations are dissociated, it can be understood that in diseases as well as under the influence of psychotropic substances, a dissociation can come about. Apart from these disturbances of expressive language, it has also been observed that the conventional symbols for conceptual contents of consciousness which are clearly present for the patient cannot, in spite of all attempts, be found, but can be copied. Thus, the pattern which formulates the acoustic symbol is intact. However, it appears that it is more easily evoked like an echolalia, while the contact with those formations is loosened or completely dissolved through which experiences are integrated and abstractions, combinations, and certain thoughts which the speaker wants to communicate are developed. One deals with still other relations if the patient cannot formulate correctly the words which are given him. In this case, evidently, patterns for words in the speech area are destroyed. Summarizing, various symptoms of motor aphasia show disturbances that have to be allocated to quite different points in the neuronal system which make contents of consciousness objective by ordered and tonal use of the muscles of speech.

To complete the symptomatology which was taken from the summarizing works of more recent observations, we want to report now on an instructive surgical case which was discussed by a neurologist (Vereecken, 1958) and was interpreted by referring to Conrad (1951). The patient had a tumor in the left frontal lobe which went far below the frontal ventricle. This tumor had been removed by carefully saving the area which was occupied by the motor speech center. When the shock had subsided, which had for a short time included inability to speak, the patient could soon say a few words without any signs of wrong formation. In the same way, tones and tone connections were correctly repeated. However, there was a definite insufficiency if the patient was asked to express the acoustic symbol which belonged to certain objects. Thus he could not name, e.g., a thermometer in words, although his answers, if pressed further, showed in a roundabout manner that he knew what a thermometer was, its purpose, and by whom it was generally employed. The defect on the one side, the ability to repeat words without mistakes on the other side, allow the interpretation that the innervation patterns that are in the motor speech center are still functioning. In the same way, the connections were still present with those neuronal representations whose activity is correlated with the expressive mood of language. On the other hand, in this case, the connections with those organs must have been interrupted which correlate with complex contents of consciousness. This sketch, which is developed from the symptomatology of biological relations, fits well into the ideas to which one comes on the basis of the individual development of speech. We hark back to former statements where we started out from the drive to use the muscles and the spontaneous use of the apparatus for phonation. The innervation which is first without any order gradually becomes so differentiated that palate, tongue, and lips are combined in a babbling. The central organization that is manifested in this way presupposes a functional contact between the central representation of the peripheral motor apparatus and a projection of tensions which come about by using the speech musculature of the organs of phonation and articulation. This sensorimotor process should probably be put on a comparatively peripheral plane, probably near the motor nuclei which we activate during speech.

The correlation of the auditory system with the apparatus for phonation and articulation was a decisive step in the development of language. The place where this functional sphere was built into the cerebral organization has to be assumed to be where the impulses from the internal ear found room to develop a multiplicity of different patterns of stimulation, as in the thalamus or, better still, in the cerebral cortex. Here neuronal organizations can develop which integrate sensations to experience, including engrams of similar experiences. Here the contents of consciousness will be controlled for their feeling tones, the neuronal correlates of which will be stimulated. By regulating thus the tonus of the speech muscles, probably in a relatively direct way, it also comes to an activation of the patterns for words and sentences. The apparatus for phonation gives out motor impulses according to an order which has been laid down during learning. According to the organization of speech, the innervation of speech is built up step by step. The motor speech center would be that place which stimulates the representatives of the muscle groups in the precentral convolution to their use for linguistic expression. The analysis of other cases of aphasia, which should be as clear as possible, will have to show how far the neuronal pattern deduced from the physiological development of the ability to speak is in accord with reality. It is not only a case of the cerebral organization of linguistic expressions, but also a matter of clearing up generally valid principles. In the same way, comparison of the symptoms of disturbed functions and of normal effects should give knowledge about the correlation between subjective experience and objective processes. Language is a biological phenomenon which is peculiarly adapted to such a program.

In sensory aphasia, there must be a disturbance in the connection between the auditory sphere and that neuronal organization which connects the acoustic symbols with other sensory spheres. The pattern which evolves gives a contribution defined by the process of learning, which in its turn correlates with a certain conception. Added to these are certain patterns which are inscribed in memory, the so-called engrams. They are ready to be activated by the desire for associative connections. A pathological disorganization of the patterns or interruptions between them and the auditory sphere must lead to a disturbance in the understanding of words.

CEREBRAL ORGANIZATION AND INTEGRATED INDIVIDUALITY

The theme that is announced by this title imposes severe restrictions on the exposition. What we know today should be many times richer in order to give a comprehensive idea about the problem that we envisage. Particularly one should know much more about the organizing principle if one wants to understand the relations of the systems which are integrated and their subjective manifestations. This being so, the reader should expect no more than a modest step in the direction of the final goal of brain research, including mental activities. The fact that present knowledge about the functional organization of the brain and its correlation with mental activities that an individual of any species can perform is still in its infancy should not, however, deter us from pressing forward in our researches as much as possible.

Following these impulses, we ask first of all what can be expected from the stimulus experiments. A general answer is given by the fact that a stimulating electrode affects only a narrow circumscript area from which systems that spread far out in breadth and depth can hardly be activated sufficiently so that one could conclude in each case the effect on the organization of the whole or at least larger parts. The prospect is all the more dismal since with the increasing complexity the functional connections are more and more conditioned; instead of unequivocal connection we observe a certain number of variants one or the other of which, according to the momentary conditions, becomes manifest. For these reasons we do not dare to use those occasional observations which we made ourselves where according to protocol the effect of the diencephalic stimulation was a "searching, looking around" which could have been due to hallucinations that were artificially produced. More important is Penfield's case (1958a), in which a patient told that after electrical stimulation in the temporal lobe he saw armed robbers and was afraid of this content of consciousness, which was due to the stimulus, as though he had really seen something. Since emotional excitation goes over into the vegetative system in a well-known way, and the response of the vegetative organization in its turn influences the further elaborations of the contents of consciousness, it can under certain circumstances come to the development of comparatively strongly accented effects which are given a certain affective tone and thus lead to a manifestation of integrated individuality. The development of such

131

rich patterns of excitation and correlated contents of consciousness must be due to a part of the brain from which reciprocal neural connections to other areas exist. The engrammed experiences, as far as they become reactivated, must have their share in these effects. It has to be assumed that such cerebral organization embraces whole groups of elements that are partly in remote regions of the brain and in different layers.

One gains important clues concerning complex connections between cerebral organization and mental life from the bilateral extirpation of the temporal lobe (Klüver and Bucy, 1938). These workers studied for a long time the normal behavior of monkeys (macaques) which they used in their experiments in order to have sufficient experience for comparison with the operated animals. Analysis of their behavior indicated that the capacity seemed lost to recognize the meaning of objects with which they were well acquainted before the operation, in spite of the fact that no gross errors in visual discrimination could be found. Klüver and Bucy deduced at the time a psychic effect, because the operated animal went without hesitation to objects which before the operation gave rise to avoidance reactions and to affective discharges. Particularly remarkable were the changed food habits. The normal animal distinguishes between edible and inedible objects just by looking at them, and reacts to them either positively or negatively. After the operation the animal grasps everything without a choice and brings it to his lips and into his mouth. Only after this tactile and gustatory control were the inedible things put aside and the edible things swallowed. From this behavior we can draw three conclusions: first, the goal-directed approach and the taking up of an object means that it is actually seen. However, the monkey without a temporal lobe is unable to compare actual experiences with those that went before, to use his former experiences. This insufficiency is particularly noticeable in the visual field, but sometimes also in the auditory system. However, the interpretation of experiences of taste is not impaired. From these relations we can also understand the pronounced tendency to take all objects to and into the mouth, for this largely compensates for the defects of visual impressions. Where the visual system is impaired in its efficiency, other sensory systems take its place, in this case the well developed so-called oral sense (Edinger).

After bilateral temporal ablations, according to Klüver and his associates, profound changes in the affective behavior are added to the symptoms of these monkeys. For instance, the operated animals, in contrast to normal ones, show symptoms neither of anxiety nor anger.

Apart from the changes in the eating habits, sometimes in the form of bulimia, the ablation of the temporal lobes has remarkable consequences in still another sector of drives. This is particularly true of sexuality, which is grossly exaggerated in heterosexual, homosexual, and autosexual activity. This syndrome cannot be produced by a lesion in any other part of the brain, by ablation of only one temporal lobe, nor by removal of the lateral cortex from one or both sides. Klüver and co-workers have also given the anatomical controls to deficiency symptoms which profoundly affect the integrated individuality, and they have given these controls in a sufficiently developed phase of secondary degeneration (Bucy and Klüver, 1955). Thus they could fulfill the condition that indirect connections could also be seen. According to the interest, which we pursue here, it would be desirable to see a direct connection between the different symptoms of psychological insufficiency and certain direct or indirect structural defects. To work out such differentiated connections, however, is only possible to a limited extent because cerebral organization does not come about by arrangement in series of various sectors but has to be understood as a result of an integration with mutual connections between different systems. To disentangle these experimentally is, at the moment, only possible *grosso modo,* that is to say, only insofar as observations after partial ablation of the temporal lobe allow it. In such a topographically selective procedure, it was shown that certain groups could be delimited (Pribram and Bagshaw, 1953).

If the lesion is restricted to that part of the temporal lobe that is close to the basal ganglia, visual acuity, size of the visual field, and the ability to make simultaneous discriminations are intact. The ability for tactile discrimination is intact. Changed, however, according to the reports, is the behavior toward gustatory stimuli that may be the reason for the changes in eating habits. Another consequence of the last-mentioned operation is an increase in the general activity and the avoiding of painful situations. If the lateral frontal lobe is also ablated, one finds a disturbance of the recent memory. Surgical removal of the middle occipito-temporal region is followed, however, by the fact that the solution of problems is disturbed in which visual discrimination plays a role. Summarizing, we should mention that these observations have been frequently confirmed by Klüver and his co-workers and are also valid for cats (Klüver, 1958).

It should be added that in man, too, the same or at least a very similar cerebral organization has been found. In at least one case in which bilateral extirpation of the temporal lobe, including large parts of the uncus and the hippocampus, could not be avoided, the syndrome found by Klüver and Bucy which has just been discussed was also found (Terzian and Dalle Ore, 1955). The patient was unable to recognize anybody postoperatively, even persons formerly known very well—not even close relatives. Affectivity was also diminished. No sense of anxiety or ire could be elicited. Furthermore, here too were the symptoms of increased sexuality, an increased drive to partake of food (bulimia), and, moreover, a profound disturbance of memory. If one looks over these results, one cannot doubt the great importance of the temporal lobe for integrated individuality. Its intactness is important for intellectual efficiency, for feelings and moods, for drives, and for vegetative functions. Considering the many observations which proved that the cortex exerts not only positive, that is, constructive performances, but largely also suppresses functions that are located at lower levels, one should expect that the manifestations of an increased eating and increased sexual drive are very likely due to a disappearance of the suppressive influence and are thus part of the picture that has been described.

An important influence on functional molding of individuality, finally, is the frontal brain, or certain parts of it. Examples are, as is well known, found in observations on men, particularly in their behavior before and after leukotomy. Results of animal experiments also can be adduced; for instance, monkeys that were aggressive are changed after surgery of the anterior cingular area so that they are remarkably tame, while monkeys that were by nature anxious lose their anxious behavior after the same operation.

Investigation by the Marchi method leads us to think that such a reversal of the spontaneous behavior, in which the polarity of feelings or the polar pattern of drives, well known to psychiatrists and psychologists, becomes manifest (Kretschmer, 1956), is part of the connection between the cingular gyrus and the anterior nucleus of the thalamus on the one side and the frontal cortex on the other side.

Some of the experimental findings which are concerned with integrated individuality can also be sequences of lesions in the hypothalamus. The profound changes these lesions can induce have partly been mentioned in another connection (pp. 47, 48). In order to be more precise, some further notes should be given in line with a presentation of a former co-worker who took up again the observation that he made at that time after he had become a psychiatrist. On the basis of notes in our protocols, and using also the films and the brain sections, the following findings have been described (W. Stoll, 1959). The preoperative character of cats was observed on the average for about two weeks. During the experiments, the exchange of gases and the temperature were controlled, also the reactions in experiments of overheating or under-cooling (Bloch, 1943; Stoll, 1943). The animals, which lived for three to twenty weeks after the experiment, were generally apathetic. However, this apathy was not so strong that the defense reaction which has been described previously was completely extinguished. The interest of the cat in its environment, the drive to orienting contacts, was definitely diminished but was not completely wiped out. Occasionally, they became exaggeratedly frightened. Gradually, there were signs of recovery from the deficient behavior due to the operation. The whole behavior, however, was still different from that before the operation. Animals that had previously been sweet and trusting became frightened and very aggressive. One also had the impression of a certain mental lability. It is probably part of the polarity of feelings that has been mentioned several times that in a few animals of the same group there occurred just the opposite change of character—cats which were wild or timid before the operation afterward became gentle and also slightly apathetic. Another animal before the operation showed a certain tendency to lean on somebody, but was not well-tempered. After the lesion of roughly symmetrical coagulations, she had still more the need to lean on somebody while she expressed her well-being by the typical purring noise.

According to Stoll (1959), all these symptoms are very much reminiscent of leukotomized patients in whom influences that normally arise in the frontal lobe are not completely used in the integration of the individuality. Apart from that, there were no immediate connections between the degree of mental change and the disturbances in the regulation of the body temperature or the general bodily conditions. On the other hand, there was undoubtedly a great similarity to diseases after limited but differently localized lesions of the brain, namely those corresponding to the local psychosyndrome of M. Bleuler. We can thus conclude that the effect of a lesion in the anterior and middle hypothalamus on the mental processes is not specific. When we keep in mind the regulation of the readiness to function of the different systems that are knitted together in the integrated organization we should expect in spite of this localization of the foci that the local psychosyndrome can be reduced to a common denominator. It could be due to a change in the balance of the endophylactic-trophotropic system by which the activity of the whole brain is subdued or inhibited by the local processes of healing.

In view of the gaps that still exist and that make the stimulation and extirpation experiment unsuited for a satisfactory understanding of individuality, experiences are welcome which are garnered in a different manner and that throw a light on the problem we now discuss. Here we use neither the stimulating electrode nor the scalpel for ablations, but a chemical instrument. Such agents that influence the psychic processes have been known for a long time on an empirical basis because they are used or misused, to a large extent, for their psychic effects. It is enough to think of alcohol, opium, and the so-called waking amines, to name but a few concrete examples.

Recently, other substances have become known that are used in neurology and psychiatry, the so-called psychopharmaca, used in the interests of the psychophysiologist for the analysis of connections between cerebral organization and pharmacological effect on the development of contents of consciousness. To get insight into the psychodynamics of the whole individual, they are particularly useful because the symptoms can be compared with those of known chemoregulators in the body. It should be added that a substance that is brought to the tissue by the blood goes to all parts and layers of the cerebral organization and can have its effect there.

To keep the connection with the symptoms that have previously been described, we mention further observations in order to get a still more comprehensive view. When we talked about the sensory performances, we talked about the fact that under the influence of very small amounts of LSD, certain errors of the visual function, among others, occur. In this connection, we refer to the work of Stoll (1947) that was mentioned on page 100 about spontaneous light seen with closed eyes which was partly of a primitive nature, partly of a simple form, and reminded subjects of formerly seen figures or natural shapes. Pictures with intellectual content can—as we said there—arise as visual contents of consciousness, even without external stimulation. An important role is played by illusions, which have to be considered as errors in the integration of exteroceptive stimuli. Parts of the former experiences were also induced and were brought in connection with actual experiences. Such phenomena signify a spreading out of the pattern elicited by exteroceptive stimuli into the memory. As the reason for such visionary contents of consciousness, we have to consider a supranormal excitation of the elements whose activity under physiological conditions somehow brings the correlated patterns to consciousness.

It appears useful to take cognizance once more of the previous detailed analysis to understand the symptomatology and its relation to cerebral organization. We inform ourselves, therefore, about further effects of LSD and first of all envisage those effects which this substance elicits in voluntary motions. According to W. Stoll, first of all we find disturbances in the precision of directed movements. If in grasping we frequently miss the object, or an object is not put in the place where it is supposed to be, this may be due to disturbances in the proprioceptivity which in a well-known manner controls the result of the motor innervation. A slight shift in the excitability of afferent stimulation must lead to error in the composition of the integral patterns of movement. Apart from this effect, a change in the threshold of the central representation of motor effectors has to be considered.

One has also to deal with disturbance brought about in this or some other way if words are spoken indistinctly or with bad articulation or if one writes sloppily with uncertainty of details. Another phenomenon that should be noted is the transposition of letters within single words. This shows that the acoustic symbols for certain ideas cannot be produced as they were learned previously. The error has hardly to be looked for in those processes by which contents of consciousness become objective as language symbols in the shape of acoustic figures. For when we speak fluently, words are formed automatically. In all likelihood, the last-named disturbance of speaking is due to errors in proprioceptivity, because the pattern of vowels and consonants is, as described before, due to the control of tension in the vocal apparatus and in the order of its movements.

A further symptom of LSD is error in intellectual functions. This is easily understood because such complicated and generally indirectly achieved goals are based on the use of perceptions reinforced by items of former experiences. Thus it can be understood that shifts in the excitability of the functioning neurons, for instance, an increase, lead to faster thought processes, sometimes with definite leaps, as has actually been observed. A lowering of the ability to concentrate, connected with an easy distractibility, belongs to the same complex of symptoms. Under these circumstances, it is hardly surprising if the ability to differentiate between important and unimportant

139

things is lowered. For in such mental performances the quantitative moment has the decisive role. This is also true for evaluating behavior in social situations, where one has to distinguish between what one may and what one may not do.

If we now turn to disturbances due to LSD in the realm of feelings and moods, a definite uncertainty about time should always be mentioned, according to Stoll. It is not easy to form any idea how this change in subjective experience is correlated with neuronal processes. One might think of a correspondence with the fast or even jerky thinking processes which were just described and which we brought in connection with the corresponding changes in the transmission of stimuli. In any case, under such circumstances, it becomes impossible to gauge the time through which one has lived.

A very queer subjective manifestation of LSD is the feeling of being outside oneself where, however, the contact with the environment does not have to be completely broken. We dare only to ask whether it might be a kind of giddiness, but we should not hesitate to point out that Penfield speaks of an electrical stimulus which gave the patient the feeling that he was far away from himself (Penfield, 1958a).

Another mental manifestation of LSD is the evocation of a euphoric mood. In the experiment, it occurs together with a desire to undertake something, as a "pasha mood," as a desire to dance, laugh, or march. Another variation is a contemplative euphoria, and in other cases again there is a positively toned apathy. The experience seems to be of importance that in none of these cases definite reasons for the mood provoked by chemical agents could be given. It also should be noted that only about half the subjects reacted in this way, whereas in the other half the mood evoked by LSD had a depressive character; fatigue was evoked, or the sensation of having been beaten, or the subject had a disagreeable feeling of being sick. If, at the same time, there was an indefinite feeling of motor excitation, there might have been a mixed form, e.g., an alternating up and down. Such different effects are of interest because they show typical differences in the psychic constitutions of individuals and also the dependence of the whole psychological and/or somatic situation in which the individual happens to be at the moment.

Another observation which is of interest concerns the correspondence between mood, mimesis, and gestures. Where the mood is a giddy one, the facial musculature is innervated accordingly and in an obligatory manner so that the person cannot repress laughter. However, he knows perfectly well that there is no reason to laugh in the situation. Depressive moods are also accompanied by a corresponding mimetic expression, as by the inclination to cry.

If one thus finds opposite modes of behavior, one has to think immediately of those experimental results in which from the same region or from certain zones which are in close contact with each other, electrical stimulations also give contrasting effects, either fleeing or repulsion by attack, either rapacious hunger or taking no food at all (see pp. 34, 38 ff.). In these cases, too, we surmise that readiness of the neurons to react was either individually different or was dependent on the general mood. It should be added that the activation of one kind of behavior always inhibits the opposite one, as one can see in the realm of the vegetative nervous system, so that as complete an accomplishment as possible is insured (Hess 1948b).

The activation or suppression of drives is, as we explained before, closely connected with moods and feelings. Thus one is not surprised that these also appear in the symptoms of LSD. In the concrete case, it is expressed by the attenuation of sexuality.

Drives very easily go over to symptoms which are connected with a vegetative function. Among these have to be considered the sweating that is occasionally observed. Now and then one also sees remarkably deep breathing. If the pharmacon is given in higher doses, one also observes a decrease in the frequency of the heart beat. Reactions of the innervation of vessels can be noticed by the pale face and red conjunctivae. From the intestinal tract, one should mention an occasional desire to vomit or to gag. How to evaluate these defects has in principle been explained previously where we differentiated between an ergotropic, or, extroverted, and an endophylactic-trophotropic attitude of the organism. The latter is a protection from overloading and a promotion of restituting processes (Hess, 1924, 1925).

According to these two life-preserving principles, we also have to judge the effects of psychotropic substances. In point of fact, such an interpretation of the symptoms of various psychopharmaca has already been made (Rothlin, 1957; Brodie, Spector and Shore, 1959; Brodie and Shore, 1957; Cerletti, 1958; Elkes, 1958; Wikler, 1957). What we ourselves have to say about this subject concerns the relativity of the relation of individual symptoms to certain physiological functions. The miosis, for instance, can be on the one side an expression of trophotropic moods, a concomitant of tiredness, still more pronounced in sleep. Also acting as a protection against overstimulation of the photoreceptors, oriented in an endophylactic-trophotropic direction, is the narrowing of the pupils. However, when the eyes converge, things are different. In this case, miosis increases the visual performance in the sense that the optic apparatus has a higher degree of resolution. Conforming to the extroverted function of the eye, this increase in performance has to be considered an ergotropic reaction. Similarly, vasoconstriction is not an unequivocal criterion for the ergotropic or the trophotropic adjustment of the organism. If the arteries in the splanchnic region become narrow, more blood flows to the muscles and the brain. With the constriction in the region of the coronary vessels is associated a sparing of the heart; that is to say, a symptom of a trophotropic adjustment. Pilo-erection too has two opposite aspects, if it is functionally interpreted. In connection with repulsion, reacting against an enemy, it is typically ergotropic, namely, a component of the threatening gesture. As the body becomes undercooled, however, the erection of the hairs is part of a defense reaction which, under such circumstances, lessens the amount of heat given off, which would be disadvantageous. These examples show that isolated effects have to be understood in their importance for the whole organism as a part of the more complete organization, and this is also true for the symptoms induced by psychotropic substances.

Another question concerns the places in which the substance exerts its influence within certain systems or groups of systems. In this respect, the elements of the various planes may have different sensitivities, which change the physiological order in different ways. Apart from that, one has to keep in mind that a certain effect may have not only direct, but indirect consequences as well. One is faced with the former possibility if the psychotropic substance immediately attacks those elements which, when agitated, become combined in a pattern correlated with the order in which they become manifest in the contents of consciousness. This is most likely in the case of visual experiences under the influence of LSD. In other words, the elementary phenomena such as dancing flames, color phenomena of indefinite shape, perhaps also the seeing of movement, may be correlated with elements of the primary visual cortex. Where definite figures are seen, or hallucinated, one could with greater justice assume that we have a response of elements of the secondary visual cortex. If the subject notices first of all the visual experiences which correspond to elements known from former experiences, we might assume that the excitations go to a layer in which the experiences are engrammed. One might think here of the fern or the benzol ring (p. 101).

Among indirectly evoked symptoms of psychotropic substances we should count those behaviors by which certain feelings and moods are expressed, as in motor expressions that are a sign of a definite desire to undertake something and in other case behavior which corresponds to the feeling of tiredness. As far as the feelings and moods themselves are concerned, their appearance has to be considered as an immediate effect, such as the excitation of the syndrome of rage after electrical stimulation of the system that has been described above, or the syndrome of anxiety together with the concomitant vegetative symptoms. These latter can come about by direct influence of the substance of the elements on the hypothalamic centers, just as in electrical stimulation. However, one also has to keep in mind the influence on the peripheral elements of the innervation apparatus in the effectors themselves. The one mechanism does not exclude the other.

It is a task of future research to analyze systematically the way in which the various psychotropic substances act on the functional organization of the brain and thereby give an experimental contribution to the demonstration of functional systems, the activity of which is correlated with contents of consciousness. A step in this direction is the stereotactic injection of biologically active substances into the brain or the ventricles, as has been done successfully by Feldberg and Sherwood (1954) and Hess (1924–25). Also, the testing of various isolated organs, perhaps also of elements in tissue cultures, may be suitable to increase our knowledge of symptoms due to psychotropic substances.

A problem of a particular kind is presented by those processes that are correlated with complex, complicated contents of consciousness that go on for some time. If Penfield could evoke by electrical stimulation in the region of the temporal lobe an experience like that of a robbery, the area with the constantly changing pattern of excitation is known, as we said before. It is easily understood that structures of the temporal lobe may also be the place on which LSD acts. The effect should be thought of as due primarily to autonomous deviations. The heightened excitability would lead to the consequence that some elements are united to patterns that may be correlated, like an illusion or hallucination, with contents of consciousness.

If we look for another substance that may be interesting from the psychophysiological point of view and that has been studied on numerous psychically sound people, we have to think of dibenamine and its symptoms. This compound, which is chemically well defined, was given intravenously to patients with high blood pressure with a somatic therapeutic goal, namely, for its sympatholytic effect, i.e., its inhibiting effect on the ergotropic system. This led, in about one-fifth of all cases (14 out of 68) to "severe psychic functional disturbances." Going back to the extensive report of the author (Walther-Buel, 1949), we shall discuss the symptomatology, again keeping in mind the organic order realized in the integrated individual which, on the basis of the observations which have been made, is largely possible. Again we begin with the effects on the organs which immediately sustain life, with those from the vegetativum. We then go over to feelings and moods as they are conditioned by somatic needs, insofar as they motivate the behavior which releases tensions. The next step leads us to the influence on the readiness of sensorimotor system, and, finally, to a drive-like co-ordination of those goal-directed movements which are under vestibular and proprioceptive control and which are governed by exteroceptive information from the sensory systems. Then we have the integration of parts of the experiences with the representation of space and time.

Here abstractions and combinations play a not unimportant role.

Following this program, we notice first the rather remarkable fact that psychic disturbances were only seen in a minority of subjects. In this restriction, the physiological scatter of the psychic individuality comes out very definitely. One finds this confirmed by the fact that when it comes to a shift in mood, this may occur in different directions. Some persons showed an unmotivated euphoria such as may occur physiologically in a milder form when the subject is in a well-attuned psychophysical balance. Such a positive feeling tone can lead to exaggerated behavior; in a concrete case, in spite of the situation, the patient wanted to embrace his nurse. The manifestation of a euphoric mood can, however, change over into an aggressive or sad mood, particularly in the last phase of a hangover. To the elementary psychic disposition is also to be added the fact that under dibenamine people become easily frightened and show a remarkable anxiety, both of which are in principle protective reactions. A change in the readiness to become spontaneously active or a change in the reactivity is present if the patient becomes unusually restless, a change which may be so strong that he can be kept in his bed only with difficulty. A particular form of increased psychomotor effect is a heightened desire to speak, resulting in senseless talking with empty words. The opposite are phases of definite psychomotor depression, during which nothing is said and the patient reacts little or not at all when addressed, often by simply winking his eye. A still more impressive suppression is a stupor.

On a higher plane in which limited contents of consciousness are ordered to a logical chain of thought, there may occur disturbances which are analogous to those which we have seen in psychomotor behavior, i.e., lack of precision. Thoughts become fleeting, the ability to concentrate is diminished, the person is easily distracted. Part of this symptomatology is the behavior in which during conversation the patient will follow everything but only quite superficially, so that the necessary correlation with the proper experience does not come about. This limiting of intellectual abilities can, under certain circumstances, go so far that what is heard is not understood in its sense but is simply repeated, as in echolalia, but here too an opposite effect has been observed, namely, an increased tendency to associative connections which can assume the experience of scenes like a pantomime. Remarkably frequently, experiences were concomitant with the feeling already known in its kind which corresponds to the déjà-vu phenomenon and which apears after electrical stimulation as well as with LSD. Psychodynamically related is probably the feeling that a certain experience is repeated several times, for instance, that the doctor or nurse who comes into the room appears in the same way time and again and gets busy with the infusion or asks the same questions repeatedly. Evidently, in such cases, the pattern of excitation which has once been engrammed perseverates by projecting back into that layer in which the exogenous influences are assimilated by the consciousness and are felt as being present.

The information is also of interest which one gets when the dibenamine effect wears off. In all cases, the feeling remains that there is or was a mental disturbance. The ability to perceive the realities of the environment was not completely lost under the influence of this drug. In differentiation to well-known toxic deliria, unequivocal hallucinations were an exception. Thus the contents of consciousness which appear after dibenamine are similar to or the same as those which appear after electrical stimulation (Penfield, 1958) or after LSD (Stoll, 1947). It may be as though under physiological conditions we are busy with certain thoughts but still roughly know where we are and what happens around us. Between activation of parts of the experiences and actual sensations there was frequently a competition, which does not mean that one excludes the other completely. The detailed analysis of these psychodynamic relations offers a promising possibility of deeper insight into the relations between experiences and actual happenings on the one side, and manifestations of former experiences on the other side. From the dynamic conception of psychic disturbances, one should expect that they would afford important clues for the understanding of normal psychic processes. Moreover, undoubted similarities between some effects of substances of different chemical structure show that psychic processes are largely dependent on cerebral organization and are stimulated or suppressed because of specific affinities. It is further important which experiences are at hand when the agents act, and whether either the somatic systems or their different members are ready to work. The same viewpoint seems to us also to be important for the relations between hormonal factors and psychic peculiarities, so that here the connections between endocrinology and psychiatry, which have been particularly emphasized by M. Bleuler (1953), fit in organically.

If in the summary one puts together the most important consequences, they are that a specific psychopharmacon which influences structures on the lowest plane, i.e., that one which is closest to the vegetative plane, becomes important for the deformation of physiological basic feelings. The whole character of the subject is changed. Effects on the properties of elements which belong to a higher plane activate more differentiated feelings and moods. Where influences on intellectual performances are present, these can either come about by modifications of the steering of the readiness to function or as a consequence of a direct influence on those elements which belong to this higher plane. Apart from the mechanism which differentiates according to planes, some members of the same plane may particularly react in either a positive or a negative direction. Finally, it may happen that several or all planes of one or several functional systems react more or less strongly, either positively or negatively, depending on the whole situation and the temporal processes. To lay down experimentally the conditions which are responsible for one or the other manner is a program that is of equal interest for psychophysiology and psychopathology. Further clues are given by the study of psychosomatic disturbances. The clinical case takes the place of a psychophysiological experiment which can hardly be duplicated so far as it is possible to establish connections between the symptomatology and the principles of the processes involved (Hess, 1961a and b).

III

REVIEW

AND

COMMENT

PSYCHODYNAMIC PRINCIPLES AND FUNCTIONAL ORGANIZATION OF THE BRAIN

In the first part of this book, we looked at forms of *behavior* which were connected with the contents of consciousness and which were subjectively experienced.

In the second part, we dealt with connections that were recognizable or even probable between *psychic performance* and the *functional organization* of the brain.

In this third part, we will try to put these two interests on a common basis. To approach a solution of the task, one has to keep in mind that in both cases one has to do with processes of experiencing, remembering, and evaluating on the one side and with processes of direct action and expressions on the other side. These several manifestations are unequivocally part of the work of the brain because of its functional organization. Thus we are led to a comparison of the governing dynamic principles in both cases in order to find out where certain correspondences can be found.

The accomplishments that were related in the first part are part of innate *endowments* to develop contents of consciousness. This ability uses information which is brought to it by the various sensory systems. When these are integrated, the

rials are the impulses which are given out by the receptors of the sensory organs if they are stimulated. The sensory organs are oriented toward differentiation. The centripetally conducted excitations become integrated to patterns or sequences of patterns.

The combinations rest on manifold *connections* that represent a number of possible patterns. The combinations occur because of the neighborhood of the excitable elements (convergence). Neighborhood connections that are functional can also be mediated by fiber tracts. The potential contents that are in this way or otherwise repeated become effective, if the elements become excited either simultaneously or in ranked succession. Successions which are only separated by very small gaps become integrated, that is to say, they become flowing patterns, which means the same as movement and change of the pattern of the figure. Contacts, which are simultaneous or follow each other rapidly, mean automatic melting together in one process in space and time.

The *excitability* of the various elements and integrating systems differs and may depend on internal states on the one side and external influences on the other side. The former vary, due to previous activity or due to factors in the environment of the neurons. In this way, hormonal, neurosecretory, or even foreign substances may cause a change of properties.

A particular role is played by the *negative induction* between the synergistic elements. In a population of synergistic elements, those come first which have the highest excitability. By responding, they give a positive contribution to the formation of patterns. At the same time, they suppress elements in their neighborhood which are less excitable. Thus the spikes of the pattern of excitability become sharp and the pattern becomes richer in contrast and therefore clearer. These processes are probably particularly pronounced in the higher planes of the sensory system.

Planes of elements which are in connection with those on which the peripheral excitations are projected have still other properties. They may even be connected with each other. The patterns and sequences of patterns are taken over and strengthened as *engrams*. A sequence of patterns that comes from the sensory organs and leads to a perception reactivates automatically similar engrams. By becoming excited they join the immediately activated and integrated patterns of excitation. In repeating identical components they become more deeply engrammed. Components that are different in shape and in temporal sequence are more or less suppressed. The youthful individual has inborn neuronal patterns, i.e., a correspondingly organized specific inheritance of patterns. Such patterns can be further developed by repeated experiences.

Excitation of *systems of opposite effect* goes hand in hand with mutual inhibition. The system with higher tension establishes itself as active. Its priority may gradually decrease and thus the suppression may cease. There may be a change of direction as far as the effect is concerned. The manifestation of organization of the brain presupposes internal tensions and spontaneous shifts in tensions. They motivate a synergistic co-ordination of motor innervation that leads to a decrease in tension and therefore approaches quietude.

Complicated co-ordinated activities do not always lead to the goal at once. By repetition, innervating patterns are evolved, the results become improved, the processes become faster, and detours are avoided. Simple patterns of activation become automatized. This occurs after many trials. The trial is connected with controls on the various planes and the movement is guided according to the principle of control of the effect, in higher accomplishments also involving the higher sensory organs. The final result is a co-ordination which always hits the goal and which is gradually achieved by repetitions. Its pattern gradually becomes organically fixed by prolonged use. In the psychic realm too, spontaneous and induced activity together with regulatory feedback and the stabilization of expressive order is a creative principle.

Motor innervation with aimed effects can be excited from the outside and from the inside, i.e., by sensory impressions as they are integrated to patterns. Similarly, under certain circumstances, processes that are due to the joining of engrams, abstractions, and combinations motivate movements and regulate them according to the goal. Movements that would collide with each other become similarly excluded by suppression so that only one, probably the one that has the greatest tension, comes off without interference.

Comparison of the psychic performances and a dynamic conception of cerebral organization shows far-reaching *correspondences*. In point of fact, the result of mental working on information is quantitatively congruent with the result of real constructions. If the builder of a bridge is guided by an idea of how he can solve the tasks given him, and constructs it according to visual control and using heard, read, and seen data as well as his own experience, his realized work corresponds with the ideas which he worked out so precisely that one can trust one's life to it without hesitance. This means that the experiences given by sensory impressions are projected somehow into the consciousness and motivate in the proper way the actions which flow from this *idea*. In a similar way, a creative chemist reaches his goal sufficiently often, if he carries through the synthesis by using all his knowledge and observations in his experiments. If he has thought and acted correctly, he finally will have a product with the looked-for properties. We should not forget the doctor who, by integrating his observations, arrives at an idea of the cause of a disturbed function and then works out a plan for healing by using his own and other, accumulated experiences. By giving the correct orders, the idea becomes realized and healing will progress. The success may not come about if he has used a wrong idea at the beginning because of factors which are not known to him or if the patient, because of peculiarities of his constitution, does not respond to the orders in the way in which most of them do.

The hint for constructive principles should also include a mention of the ability to *repair autonomously* defects of patterns which may be either sensory or motor. If this has to do with the reorganization of members in parallel, it corresponds to the principle of compensation. If supra-ordinated members of a system fall out, subordinated members in the organization may repair the defective function.

Concerning *topology* as a principle of structure and function, and the role of symbolism and the importance of a large number of elements and their connections, we can refer the reader to page 21. The principles that rest on these things are valid for the development of contents of consciousness as well as for the functional organization of the brain. The number is thus important on the one side for a regulation of the intensity of a transmitted stimulus, and on the other side for a very large, in the case of the brain an almost infinite, number of combinations.

FORCES OF ORDER

If the physiologist goes beyond his special interests and turns to modern work on information theory, he will make contact with cybernetics. Here we find out more about apparatus which when used will lead to accomplishments that used to be reserved to the human brain or perhaps to those of some animals. Under this impression, the term "electronic brain" was given currency. Although this expression is really too high, there are, nonetheless, good reasons to compare the apparatus with biology. We think, among other things, of an electrical mechanical apparatus that was developed by W.

Grey Walter (1951). In important aspects it behaves like a living being, concretely like a turtle.

This model is able, among other things, to stabilize the internal milieu by searching out the place where the necessary electric tension is renewed by recharging. On the other hand, it can also establish an equilibrium with the environment. Thus the apparatus "simulates" the elementary performance of perseveration and does what is common to all large animals. Such models can be built for very many more complicated performances and a whole science has been developed which teaches successfully new tasks which are remembered and gives excellent services to modern man in industry, science, and economy, and even in exchanging ideas. Because of these goals, N. Wiener introduced the word "cybernetics." It defines the science which deals with regulation, or governing, and with information, as far as these things are common to living beings and technical apparatus. To illustrate this concept still further, we base ourselves on a lecture that was given by a leading cyberneticist to a biological audience (Hovland, 1960). He reported on apparatus that can be brought, by repeating a certain task, to solve this task quicker and with greater precision. We have to deal with an effect, therefore, which is normally due to learning. A well known analogue, according to Pavlov, is the training of a dog to a conditioned reaction, but more complicated patterns of stimuli can also be worked over, so that a dominant feature becomes registered among them. When properly adjusted, the same reaction comes about if the apparatus is given a number of different figures, e.g., a triangle—large or small—with an obtuse or an acute angle. The apparatus chooses a certain criterion from several combinations. It does in principle the same as man, who has learned to recognize figures of a certain category.

A further analogue to a comparatively high form of learning is realized in a program which, after exercising the rules of a game such as checkers for ten to twenty hours, uses the experiences made during that time in such a way that among all possible moves, the one is made that has the greatest chance to win. The apparatus can reach levels of performance that are comparable to those of an excellent human player.

Still more remarkable is the performance of an apparatus that performs the functions of a translator. In this case, we are not offered, for example, for a German word a Russian word as it is taken from the dictionary. From among several expressions which, according to the context, have a different meaning, the cybernetic apparatus chooses the one that gives the right meaning in just this context. The apparatus has, therefore, engrams, that is to say, score patterns that are equivalent to a learned sequence of words that have meaning. Whoever might be inclined to dismiss this faculty as not comparable should keep in mind that the communication between men, as was described earlier, also works only with patterns or symbols. Only in this case they consist of combinations of impulse patterns that are transmitted through air and are spoken or heard as contents or as a sequence or words. The patterns themselves, as we pointed out there, have no causal connection to the transmitted content of consciousness. The association is merely empirical because we learn to use a language under actual conditions. The learning apparatus is in an analogous position. In it, as in man, the important thing is the functions of the pattern to find the learned pattern after a given word by paying attention to the sequence of words and to give the translation, as an answer. Seen merely in the abstract, the problems are the same whether engrammed combinations of patterns and sequences of combinations are given by a neuronal apparatus or electromagnetically.

Some reader may wonder how these patterns can be worked over. To mention it briefly and to satisfy any possible interest, it may be said that the task given the apparatus is fed into the apparatus by a set pattern of holes or as symbols of a certain type on a piece of paper and that in their working vacuum tubes or transistors are used to magnetize drums, or other magnetic gadgets, to fix the engrams for later evocation. All the rest is a matter of combinations as they are given on the perforated tape and as they become realized by electrical currents. We also have here an electromechanical arrangement that is used to make holes in patterns in the tape, which are symbols that are used as a language to give a task. If it is solved, the machine receives the answer in the form of symbolic letters.[1]

What is particularly important to a psychophysiologist, apart from analogous performances, concerns the way in which electromagnetic arrangements work. There are only two possibilities, a yes or a no. When these are combined, there results a great number of patterns that lead to a solution. We have the same relations in the structure of the cerebral organization, whose elements become either activated or inhibited. For this reason, the working out of information comes about by combinations between the neurons that lead to the translation of the incoming information to the output as an answer. What carries the abstracted order and the combined forces here or there is irrelevant. According to the processes that have been described, the familiarity with the working of cybernetic apparatus gives the biologist, including zoologists and medical men who are interested in the brain, a unique help. By getting to know the cybernetic apparatus and their way of working when they have to learn certain tasks, we have concrete possibilities for functional comparison of the model with the brain that is made out of neurons. That the "electronic

---

[1] The author wants to express his thanks to Mr. T. Richard from the Institute for Telephone Technique at the Eidgenössische Technische Hochschule, Zürich. This man, who is interested in cybernetics, afforded the author an opportunity to see the structure of an electrical computer with proper explanations and thus to gain a picture of the various organs, their arrangement, and their function.

brain" has to be operated with a man-made program in order to work meaningfully is the important difference and sufficient reason to avoid the word "brain." If, beside the possibilities that are in the apparatus, other ways of working can also be thought of, we nonetheless get a sharper idea about organic functions. In point of fact, brain research will do without a stimulating help if it bypasses the methodology, possibilities, and results of cybernetics.

It is hardly necessary to point out that an entirely different subject is treated, if we ask how the neuronal information becomes conscious. We go back to an example given in the first part, if we remind the reader that a physically defined sequence of tones, as on an organ or a sequence of pictures projected on the screen is transformed into certain contents of consciousness. Our inability to picture the translation of neuronal into psychic processes causally does not change the fact of correlation—as we already pointed out in the former context. Obviously, from the auditive ideas of an artist who plays without notes, plus or minus impulses go out that activate the muscles without error through whose co-ordination the musical composition becomes objective and can be heard. Then the tonal figures of the organ stimulate as physical processes the receptors in the inner ear. As nervous impulses, they are propagated and worked into patterns which then become manifest in the contents of consciousness. Although one is at the moment still not sure exactly where the motor impulses originate, it is impossible that they could become realized without a pattern arising in consciousness.

Here we have another constructive idea. If we say that in a mental process, a content of consciousness is translated into a co-ordinated pattern of impulses that corresponds to a certain drive, we presuppose that somehow some forces are involved. This raises a delicate problem, at least insofar as one discusses its essence. However, it is easy to define force as a concept, to define the conditions under which it becomes manifest, and to describe its effects. To go back to the first problem, it can be said that there are several types of force. We might remind the reader that one of these was only found recently, namely, that one which leads to the connection of nucleons in the nucleus of the atom. Another one is the type of electromagnetic forces that are effective, for instance, between the nucleus and the electrons in an atom. Still a different kind of force is gravitation. The question arises to which category belong the psychic forces that are responsible for the excitation and coordination of muscle forces. How hunger and thirst signify motivating tensions has been said. It is doubtful, however, whether these tensions belong to any of the categories just mentioned. We do not know anything that could speak for that. What is clear, however, concerns the character of neuronal systems. These are connected with the ontogeny of living beings because in the first stages of the earth there were no adequate conditions for the existence of living beings. Even today the serious problem of the origin and drives of life has not been solved. The forms and abilities that belong to animals and men must have been developed during their evolution.

Considering that there are different categories of forces in connection with different structures, it could be asked whether psychic performances belong to the manifestation of a particular type of force. Here it would be possible to discuss certain ideas that are widely disseminated. We have no time for that, however, and can only want to refer to works which discuss them (Kornmüller, 1955; Picha, 1958). Apart from that, we let the enigmatic be an enigma and concern ourselves exclusively with the constatation of correlation between neuronal and psychic processes.

161

CONCLUSION

In the literature, one talks here and there about the "seat" of consciousness. Arguments are adduced that it should be located in the brain stem. That the brain stem is involved in the formulation of contents of consciousness is very likely. Our own experimentation on the diencephalon points in that direction. An exclusive correlation can, however, hardly be vindicated. We ourselves think that ganglion cells of different kinds, as they are described in different places, contribute to it. Of decisive importance are the connections, vertical as well as horizontal. Some observations speak for the assumption that, according to the contents of consciousness, different formations in different planes may be involved. One has to assume that elementary feelings and moods gravitate toward the rostral portions of the brain stem. When we deal, however, with the large number of details, we think that the broadly laid-out formations as they occur in various parts of the cortex play a role, although the ability to experience complete and flowing contents of consciousness is in principle bound to the brain as a whole, with changing participation of the different structures from content to content.

Finally, the question remains open of what is the physiological importance of psychic endowment of living beings, the ability to feel, to perceive, to remember, to form ideas, to abstract, to combine, or to act in a goal-directed manner. In spite of unsolved riddles, how the correlation between contents of consciousness and neuronal processes comes about, the answer is clear. One can take it from the first part of this work and we do not have to do more here than quite generally mention once more the role of these abilities for the preservation of individual existence and of the species. Through the performance of the sensory system and synergistically co-ordinated motor innervation, an individual becomes conscious of a source of food, and is led to it, particularly in connection with memory. Much of the time, he is also able to avoid threatening danger or actively to oppose it. Compare with this the mental impossibility, as of a man in coma, in unconsciousness, in narcosis, or in deep sleep, to protect himself. The subjective reconstruction of objective data occurs on the basis of stimuli and of integration as well as of the realization of individual drives that become systematized, to a large extent independently of mere chance. This does not mean that in the development of regulatory dispositions, chance cannot play the role of a constructive factor. In man, with his highly developed interests, these relations may not always be so obvious, for frequently enough he tries to find a fulfillment of his tensions in an indirect way and these cannot always be recognized by the observer, particularly when they are directed to a distant goal. Added to these are motives of a particular kind that refer to feelings and emotions and stimulate individuals who are gifted in a certain area. We think here of aesthetic experiences which one sees objectively, to remain at the simplest level, in ornamentation of prehistoric objects or among primitive people, as rhythm, in the movement of the body, or in acoustic expressions. The analysis of inborn motives of the aesthetic experience shows a relation to order, namely, to symmetry, to a stable structure, and to regular proportions (Hess, 1952c; Weiss, 1955; Weyl, 1952). Oratorical euphony also results from the connections between the elements of the composition. From a biological viewpoint, it is of principal interest that ordered structure is of importance for the integrated comprehension of a great number of elements, because it corresponds to the principles of the functional organization of the brain. This interpretation is even valid where the inborn Anlagen are further developed by experiences, in some cases so far that whoever is less gifted and less trained in that particular field, cannot follow, and reacts with a negative feeling tone.

In going beyond the area specifically mentioned above, one is led to the conclusion that the content of subjective experience is bound to the structure of the brain and the properties of its structural elements and that only those contents of consciousness can be developed that correspond to the organization of the brain.

BIBLIOGRAPHY

A

Publications Used in the Text

Adey, W. R.: The sense of smell. Hdb. Physiol. Section I: Neurophysiology. Vol. 1, *535* Amer. Physiol. Soc. Washington, 1959.

Akert, K.: Der visuelle Greifreflex. Helvet. physiol. pharmacol. Acta 7 (1949), 112.

Akert, K., B. Andersson: Experimenteller Beitrag zur Physiologie des Nucleus caudatus. Acta physiol. Scand. *22* (1951), 281.

Akert, K., W. Koella, R. Hess jun.: Sleep produced by electrical stimulation of the thalamus. Amer. J. Physiol. *168* (1952), 260.

Anand, B. K., J. R. Brobeck: Hypothalamic control of food intake in rats and cats. Yale J. Biol. *24* (1951), 123.

Andersson, B.: The effect of injections of hypertonic NaC1-solutions into different parts of the hypothalamus of goats. Acta physiol. Scand. *28* (1953), 188.

Andersson, B., S. M. Mc Cann: A further study of polydipsia evoked by hypothalamic stimulation in the goat. Acta physiol. Scand. *33* (1955), 333.

Andersson, S., B. E. Gernandt: Cortical projection of vestibular nerve in Cat. Acta oto-laryng., Stockholm suppl. 116 (1954), 10.

Andersson, B., W. Wyrwicka: The elicitation of a drinking motor conditioned reaction by electrical stimulation of the hypothalamic drinking area in the goat. Acta physiol. Scand. *41* (1957), 194.

Andersson, B., P. A. Jewell, S. Larsson: An appraisal of the effects of diencephalic stimulation of conscious animals in terms of normal behaviour. Ciba Foundation Symposium: Neurological basis of behaviour. Churchill, London 1958, 76.

Bächler, H.: Die ersten Bewohner der Schweiz. Francke A.G., Bern, Sammlung Dalp, *43*, 1947.

Bard, Ph.: On emotional expression after decortication with some remarks on certain theoretical views. Psychol. Rev. *41* (1934), 309, part I; *41* (1934), 424, part II.

Bard, Ph.: The hypothalamus and sexual behaviour. Res. Publ. Ass. Nerv. Ment. Dis., N. Y. *20* (1940), 551.

Bard, Ph., D. McK. Rioch: A study of four cats deprived of neocortex and additional portions of the forebrain. Johns Hopkins Hosp. Bull. *60* (1937), 73.

Bates, J. A. V.: Can voluntary movement be localised in the cerebral cortex? Brit. Assoc. Sc., Physiol. Sect., Oxford 1954.

Batini, C., G. Moruzzi, M. Palestini, G. F. Rossi, A. Zanchetti: Effects of complete pontine transections on the sleep-wakefulness rhythm: The midpontine pretrigemial preparation. Arch. biol. *97* (1959), 1.

Bättig, K., H. E. Rosvold: Psychophysiologische Leistungsfähigkeit des Macacus-Affen nach Cortexausschaltungen. Ergebnisse der Physiologie, biologischen Chemie und experimentellen Pharmakologie. 1962.

Bay, E.: Der gegenwärtige Stand der Aphasieforschung. Fol. phoniatr. *4* (1952), 9.

von Békésy, G.: Direct observation of the vibrations of the cochlear partition under microscope. Acta oto-laryng. *42* (1952), 197.

Benjamin, R. M., K. Akert: Cortical and thalamic areas involved in taste discrimination in the albino rat. J. Comp. Neurol. *111* (1959), 231.

Benjamin, R. M., C. Pfaffmann: Cortical localization of taste in Albino rat. J. Neurophysiol. *18* (1955), 56.

Bleuler, M.: Endokrinologie und Psychiatrie. Schweiz. Arch. Neurol. *71* (1953), 360.

Bloch, W.: Beziehungen des Hypothalamus zum respiratorischen Stoffwechsel. Helv. Physiol. Acta *1* (1943), 53.

Brain, W. R.: Aphasia, Apraxia and Agnosia. In: Wilson, K.: Neurology, Vol. III, p. 1413. Butterworth, London 1955.

Brodie, B. B., P. A. Shore: Mechanism of action of psychotropic drugs. Psychopharmacology Frontiers Little Brown & Co., Boston 1959. Symposium of the second International Congress of Psychiatry (1957).

Brodie, B. B., S. Spector, P. A. Shore: Interaction of Drugs with Norepinephrine in the Brain. Pharmacol. Rev. *11*/I (1959), 548.

Brooks, C. McC., D. N. Marine, E. F. Lambert: A study of the food-feces ratios and of the oxygen consumption of albino rats during various phases of experimentally produced obesity. Amer. J. Physiol. *147* (1946), 717.

von Brücke, E. Th., S. Oinuma: Über die Wirkungsweise der fördernden und hemmenden Nerven. Pflügers Arch. Physiol. *136* (1910), 502.

Brügger, M.: Fresstrieb als hypothalamisches Symptom. Helv. physiol. pharmacol. Acta *1* (1943), 183.

Bucy, P. C., H. Klüver: An anatomical investigation of the temporal lobe in the monkey (Macaca mulatta). J. Comp. Neurol. *103* 1955), 151.

Bustamente, M.: Experimentelle Untersuchungen über die Leistungen des Hypothalamus, besonders bez. der Geschlechtsreifung. Arch. Psychiatr. *115* (1943), 419.

Bustamente, M., H. Spatz, E. Weisschedel: Die Bedeutung des Tuber cinereum für das Zustandekommen der Geschlechtsreifung. Dtsch. med. Wschr. *68* (1942), 289.

Butler, T. C., I. T. Diamond, W. D. Neff: Frequency discrimination after ablation of cortical projection areas of the auditory system. J. Neurophysiol. *20* (1957), 108.

Cannon, W. B.: Bodily changes in pain, hunger, fear and rage. 2nd ed. Appleton, New York 1929.

Cerletti, A.: Biochemie, Physiologie und Pharmakologie des 5-Hydroxytryptamins (Serotonin, Enteramin). Helvet. med. Acta *25* (1958), 330.

Ciba Found. Symposium. The Nature of Sleep. Churchill, London 1961.

Cole, J., P. Glees: Effects of small lesions in sensory cortex in trained monkeys. J. Neurophysiol. *17* (1954), 1.

Conrad, K.: Aphasie, Agnosie, Apraxie. Fortschr. Neurol. *19* (1951), 291.

Critchley, M.: The parietal lobes. E. Arnold & Co., London 1953.

Denny-Brown, D., E. H. Botterell: The motor functions of the agranular frontal cortex. The frontal lobes. Proc. Ass. Res. Nerv. Ment. Dis. *27* (1948), 235.

Diesel, E.: Diesel—der Mensch, das Werk, das Schicksal. Reclam, Stuttgart 1953.

Dusser de Barenne, J. G.: Recherces expérimentales sur les fonctions du système nerveux central, faites en particulier sur deux chats dont le neopallium avait été enlevé. Arch néerl. physiol. *4* (1920), 30.

Elkes, J.: Drug effects in relation to receptor specificity within the brain: Some evidence and provisional formulation. Ciba Found. Symposium: Neurological basis of behaviour, 303. Churchill, London 1958.

Feldberg, W., S. L. Sherwood: Behaviour of cats after intraventricular injections of eserine and DFP. J. Physiol. 125 (1954), 488.

Fischel, W.: Zur Psychologie des Haushundes. Die Naturwissenschaften, 31. Jahrg. (1943), 159.

French, G. M.: Locomotor effects of regional ablations of frontal cortex in Rhesus monkeys. J. Comp. Physiol. Psychol. 52 (1959), 18.

Gemelli, A., G. Pastori: I metodi della elettroacustica nello studio del linguaggio. in: Contributi del laboratorio di Psicologia. Publicazioni della Università Cattolica del Sacro Cuore, Ser. 6, "Vita e Pensiero," Milano 8 (1935), 105.

Gemelli, A., G. G. Sacerdote, G. Bellussi: Nuovi contributi elettroacustici allo studio del canto. Comment. Pontif. Acad. Sc. 17 (1955), 1.

Glees, P.: Die Organisation der motorischen Rinde. Dtsch. Zschr. Nervenhk. 175 (1956), 155.

Glees, P., J. Cole, C. W. M. Whitty, H. Cairns: The effects of lesion in the cingular gyrus and adjacent areas in monkeys. J. Neurol., London 13 (1950a) 178.

Glees, P., J. Cole, E. G. T. Liddell, C. G. Phillips: Beobachtungen über die motorische Rinde des Affen (Rhesus, Popio strepitus und Papio papio). Arch. Psychiatr. 185 (1950b) 675.

Gloor, P.: Electrophysiological studies on the connections of the amygdaloid nucleus in the cat. Part I: The neuronal organization of the amygdaloid projection system. Electroencephalogr. 7 (1955), 223. Part II: The Electrophysiological Properties of the Amygdaloid Projection System. Electroencephalogr. 7 (1955), 243.

Goldstein, K.: Language and language disturbances. Grune and Stratton, New York 1948.

Goltz, F.: Der Hund ohne Grosshirn. Pflügers. Arch. Physiol. 51 (1892), 570.

Grey, W. W.: An electro-mechanical-animal. Biblioth. Scie. 22, Griffon, Neuchâtel 1951.

Grimm, H.: Schlafstellung und Umgebungstemperatur bei der Hauskatze, Felis catus L. Zool. Garten (NF) 22 (1956), 171.

Harlow, H. F., P. H. Settlage: Effect of extirpation of frontal areas upon learning performance of monkeys. The frontal lobes. Res. Publ. Ass. Nerv. Ment. Dis. *27* (1948), 446.

Hassler, R.: Die zentralen Apparate der Wendebewegungen. I. Ipsiversive Wendungen durch Reizung einer direkten vestibulo-thalamischen Bahn im Hirnstamm der Katze. Arch. Psychiatr. *194* (1956a), 456.

Hassler, R.: Die zentralen Apparate der Wendebewegungen. II. Die neuronalen Apparate der vestibulären Korrekturwendungen und der Adversivbewegungen. Arch. Psychiatr. *194* (1956b), 381.

Hassler, R.: Die zentralen Systeme des Schmerzes. Acta neurochir. *8* (1960), 353.

Hassler, R., T. Riechert: Klinische und anatomische Befunde bei stereotaktischen Schmerzoperationen im Thalamus. Arch. Psychiatr. *200* (1959), 93.

Hassler, R., T. Riechert: Wirkungen der Reizungen und Koagulationen in den Stammganglien bei stereotaktischen Hirnoperationen. Nervenarzt *32* (1961), 97.

Hediger, H.: Beobachtungen zur Tierpsychologie im Zoo und im Zirkus. Reinhardt A.G. Basel 1961.

Hess, W. R.: Die reflektorische Ruhigstellung schmerzender Körperteile. Arch. Physiol. *203* (1924), 539.

Hess, W. R.: Über die Wechselbeziehungen zwischen psychischen und vegetativen Funktionen. Schweiz. Arch. Neurol. *15* (1924), 260, *16* (1925), 36 u. 285.

Hess, W. R.: The mechanism of sleep. Amer. J. Physiol. *90* (1939), 386.

Hess, W. R.: Die Methodik der lokalisierten Reizung und Ausschaltung subkortikaler Hirnabschnitte. Beiträge zur Physiologie des Hirnstammes. I. Teil. Georg Thieme Verlag, Leipzig, 1932.

Hess, W. R.: Die Motorik als Organisationsproblem. Biolog. Zentralblatt, *61*, (1941), 545.

Hess, W. R.: Induzierte Störungen der optischen Wahrnehmung. Nervenarzt *16* (1943a), 57.

Hess, W. R.: Von den Gefühlen und Stimmungen eines Hundes (Ein Beitrag zur vergleichenden Psychophysiologie). Zschr. vergl. Physiol. *30* (1943b), 123.

Hess, W. R.: Das Schlafsyndrom als Folge diencephaler Reizung. Helvet. physiol. pharmacol. Acta *2* (1944), 305.

Hess, W. R.: Korrespondierende Symptome aus Stirnhirn, innerer Kapsel und vorderem Thalamus. Helvet. physiol. pharmacol. Acta *6* (1948a), 731.

Hess, W. R.: Die Organisation des vegetativen Nervensystems. Schwabe, Basel, 1948b.

Hess, W. R.: Symposion über das Zwischenhirn. Helvet. physiol. pharmacol. Acta. Suppl. VI (1950).

Hess, W. R.: Methodische Erfahrungen über die experimentelle Erforschung des Zentralnervensystems. Helvet. physiol. pharmacol. Acta 9 (1951), 367.

Hess, W. R.: Experimentalphysiologie und psychologie. Helvet. physiol. pharmacol. Acta *10* (1952 a), 85.

Hess, W. R.: Vom Lichtreiz zur bildhaften Wahrnehmung. Helvet. physiol. pharmacol. Acta *10* (1952 b), 395.

Hess, W. R.: Physiologische Grundlagen der Ästhetik. Helvet. physiol. pharmacol. Acta *10* (1952 c), 462.

Hess, W. R.: Das Zwischenhirn, Syndrome, Lokalisationen, Funktionen. Zweite, erweiterte Auflage. Benno Schwabe Verlag, Basel, 1954 a.

Hess, W. R.: The diencephalic sleep centre. In: Brain Mechanisms and Consciousness. Symposium, 117. Blackwell, Oxford, 1954 b.

Hess, W. R.: Hypothalamus und Thalamus. Experimental-Dokumente. Georg Thieme Verlag, Stuttgart 1956. (Bilderatlas mit deutsch. und engl. Legenden.)

Hess, W. R.: Psychophysiology and psychopharmacology. Neuro-Psychopharmacol. *2* (1961 a), 3.

Proceedings of the second meeting of the collegium internationale neuro-psychopharmacologium, Basel 1960. Ed. E. Rothlin. Elsevier, Amsterdam 1961.

Hess, W. R.: Die physiologische Grundlage der Psychosomatik. Dtsch. med. Wschr. *86* (1961 b), 3.

Hess, W. R.: Schlaf, sein Mechanismus und seine physiologische Funktion. Naturwiss. Rundschau *14*, (1961 c), 1.

Hess, W. R.: M. Brügger: Das subkortikale Zentrum der affektiven Abwehrreaktion. Helvet. physiol. pharmacol. acta *1* (1943 a), 33.

Hess, W. R., M. Brügger: Der Miktions- und Defäkationsakt als Erfolg zentraler Reizung im Zwischenhirn. Helvet. physiol. pharmacol. Acta *1* (1943 b), 533.

Hess, W. R., A. E. Meyer: Triebhafte Fellreinigung der Katze als Symptom diencephaler Reizung. Helvet. physiol. pharmacol. Acta *14* (1956), 397.

Hetherington, A. W., S. W. Ranson: Hypothalamic lesions and adiposity in the rat. Anat. Rec. *78* (1940), 149.

BIBLIOGRAPHY

v. Holst, E.: Neue Gedanken und Versuche zur Sensomobilität. Acta neuroveget. *12* (1955), 337.

v. Holst, E.: Die Auslö sung von Stimmungen bei Wirbeltieren durch "punktförmige" elektrische Erregung des Stammhirns. Naturwissenschaften *44,* (1957), 549.

v. Holst, E., U. v. Saint Paul: Vom Wirkungsgefüge der Triebe. Naturwissenschaften *47* (1960), 409.

Hoessly, G. F.: Über optisch induzierte Blickbewegungen. Helvet. physiol. pharmacol. Acta *5* (1947), 333.

Hovland, C.: Über die Bedeutung elektronischer Stimulatoren für die Erforschung des Verhaltens und Denkens. Rias, Berlin, 23. 11. 1960.

Hubel, D. H., T. N. Wiesel: Receptive fields, binocular interaction and functional architecture in the cat's visual cortex. J. Physiol. *160* (1962), 106.

Hunsperger, R. W.: Affektreaktionen auf elektrische Reizung im Hirnstamm der Katze. Helvet. physiol. pharmacol. Acta *14* (1956), 70.

Jung, R.: Correlation of bioelectrical and autonomic phenomena with alterations of consciousness and arousal in man. In: Brain Mechanisms and Consciousness. Blackwell, Oxford 1954.

Jung, R.: Selbstreizung des Gehirns in Tierversuch. Die Bedeutung des "self stimulation experiments" für die Neurophysiologie und Hirnlokalisation von Triebmechanismen und von Medikamentwirkungen. Parallelen und Unterschiede zum Suchtverhalten. Dtsch. med. Wschr. *83* (1958), 1716.

Jung, R.: Microphysiologie corticaler Neurone: Ein Beitrag zur Koordination der Hirnrinde und des visuellen Systems. Proc. 2. Internat. Meet. Neurobiol. Amsterdam 1959: Structure and function of the cerebral cortex. E. Tower and Schadé. Elsevier, Amsterdam 1960.

Jung, R., O. Creutzfeldt, G. Baumgartner: Microphysiologie des neurones corticaux: processus de coordination et d'inhibition du cortex optique et moteur. Colloques Internat. Centre Nat. Rech. Sc. *67* (1952), 411.

Jung, R.: Korrelationen von Neuronentätigkeit und Sehen. In: Neurophysiologie und Psychophysik des visuellen Systems: R. Jung and H. Kornhuber. Springer-Verlag, Heidelberg 1961, p. 410.

Kalischer, O.: Das Grosshirn der Papageien in anatomischer und physiologischer Beziehung. Physikal. Abhandl. Königl. Preuss. Akad. Wiss. Berlin, 1905: Abh. IV, 105 pp.

Keidel, W. D., M. E. Wigand, U. O. Keidel: Lautheitseinfluss auf die

171

Informationsverarbeitung beim binauralen Hören des Menschen. Pflügers Arch. Physiol. *270* (1960 a), 370.

Keidel, W. D.: Die Funktionsweise des menschlichen Gehörs. Umschau *60* (1960 b), 73.

Klüver, H.: Brain mechanisms and behavior with special reference to the Rhinencephalon. J. Lancet *72* (1952), 567.

Klüver, H.: "The Temporal Lobe Syndrome" produced by bilateral ablations. Ciba Found. Symp. Neurological Basis om Behaviour. Churchill, London 1958.

Klüver, H., P. C. Bucy: An analysis of certain effects of bilateral temporal lobectomy in the rhesus monkey, with special reference to "phychic blindness." J. Psychol. *5* (1938), 33.

Koehler, O.: Die Beziehung Mensch-Tier. Verhandl. Schweiz. Naturforsch. Ges. 1960, 44.

Köhler, W.: Intelligenzprüfungen an Menschenaffen. Springer-Verlag, Berlin 1921.

Konorski, J.: Conditioned reflexes and Neuron Organization. Univ. Press, Cambridge 1948.

Konorski, J.: The physiological approach to the problem of recent memory. In: Brain mechanisms and learning. Symposium Council Internat. Organiz. Med. Sc. Blackwell, Oxford 1961.

Kornmüller, A. E.: Zur Beziehung zwischen Psyche, Gehirn und Natur im Zusammenhang mit dem Naturbild der modernen Physik. Naturwiss. Rundschau *8* (1955), 140.

Kretschmer, E.: Medizinische Psychologie. 11th ed. G. Thieme, Stuttgart 1956.

Krogh, A., J. Lindhard: Regulation of the respiration and circulation during the initial stages of muscular works. J. Physiol. *47* (1913), 112.

Landgren, S.: Cortical reception of cold impulses from the tongue of the cat. Convergence of tactile, thermal, and gustatory impulses on single cortical cells. Acta physiol. Scand. *40* (1957), 202, 210.

Liddell, E. G. T.: The excitable motor cortex. Brit. Ass. Sc. Physiol. Sect., Oxford, Sept. 1954.

Lilly, J. C.: Correlations between neurophysiological activity in the cortex and short-term behaviour in the monkey. In: Biological and Biochemical Bases of Behavior. Symposium edited by H. F. Harlow and C. N. Woolsey, University of Wisconsin Press 1958.

Lilly, J. C., R. B. Cherry: Surface movements of click responses from acoustic cerebral cortex of cat: leading and trailing edges of a response figure. J. Neurophysiol. *17* (1954), 521.

Lögler, P.: Versuche zur Frage des "Zähl"-Vermögens an einem Graupapagei und Vergleichsversuche an Menschen. Zeitschr. für Tierpsychol. *16*, 2 (1959), 179.

MacLean, P. D.: Psychosomatic disease and the "visceral brain." Psychosomat. Med. *11* (1949), 338.

MacLean, P. D.: Chemical and electrical stimulation of hippocampus in unrestrained animals. Arch. Neurol. Psychiatr. *78* (1957), 113.

MacLean, P. D.: Contrasting functions of limbic and neocortical systems of the brain and their relevance to psychophysiological aspects of medicine. Amer. J. Med. *25* (1958 a), 611.

MacLean, P. D.: The limbic system with respect to self-preservation and the preservation of the species. J. Nerv. Ment. Dis. *127* (1958 b), 1.

MacLean, P. D., J. M. R. Delago: Electrical and chemical stimulation of frontotemporal portion of limbic system in the waking animal. Electroencephalogr. *5* (1953), 91.

MacLean, P. D., D. W. Ploog, B. W. Robinson: Circulatory effects of limbic stimulation, with special reference to the male genital organ. Physiol. Rev. *40*, suppl. 4 (1960), 105.

Magnus, R.: Die Körperstellung. Springer, Berlin 1924.

Meyer, R. D., H. F. Harlow, P. H. Settlage: A survey of delayed response performance by normal and brain damaged monkeys. J. Comp. Physiol. Psychol. *44* (1951), 17.

Meyer, D. R., C. N. Woolsey: Effects of localized cortical destruction on auditory discriminative conditioning in cat. J. Neurophysiol. *15* (1952), 149.

Meyer, A. E., W. H. Hess: Diencephal ausgelöstes Sexualverhalten und Schmeichlen bei der Katze. Helvet. physiol. pharmacol. Acta *15* (1957), 401.

Mishkin, M., K. H. Pribram: Analysis of the effects of frontal lesions in monkeys: II. Variations of delayed response. J. Comp. Physiol. Psychol. *49* (1956), 36.

Miller, N. E.: Experiments on motivation. Studies combining psychological, physiological and pharmacological techniques. Science *126* (1957), 1271.

Minkowski, M.: Experimentelle Untersuchungen über die Beziehungen der Grosshirnrinde und der Netzhaut zu den primären optischen

Zentren, besonders zum Corpus geniculatum externum. Habilitationsschrift, Univ. Zürich. Verlag Bergmann, Wiesbaden 1913.

de Molina, A. F., R. W. Hunsperger: Central representation of affective reactions in forebrain and brain stem: electrical stimulation of amygdala, stria terminalis, and adjacent structures. J. Physiol. 145 (1959), 251.

Moruzzi, G.: The functional significance of the ascending reticular system. Arch. ital. biol. 96 (1958), 17.

Moruzzi, G., H. W. Magoun: Brain stem reticular formation and activation of the EEG. Electroencephalogr. 1 (1949), 455.

Moruzzi, G., G. F. Rossi, A. Zanchetti: Recenti contributi alla fisiogia del sonno. (Symposium sull sonno.) Atti Soc. lombard. sc. med. 13 (1958), suppl. p. 532.

Neff, W. D., I. T. Diamond: The neural basis of auditory discrimination. In: Biological and Biochemical Bases of Behavior. Edited by H. F. Harlow and C. N. Woolsey. University of Wisconsin Press 1958.

Nielsen, J. M.: Agnosia, Apraxia, Aphasia. Their Value in Cerebral Localization. P. B. Hoeber, Inc., New York 1946.

Olds, J., P. Milner: Positive reinforcement produced by electrical stimulation of septal areas and other regions of the rat brain. J. Comp. Physiol. Psychol. 47 (1954), 419.

Parmeggiani, P. L.: Reizeffekte aus Hippocampus und Corpus mammillare der Katze. Helvet. physiol. pharmacol. acta 18 (1960), 523.

Penfield, W.: Studies of the cerebral cortex of Man—a review and an interpretation. Brain Mechanisms and Consciousness, p. 284. Blackwell, Oxford 1954 a.

Penfield, W.: Mechanisms of voluntary movement. Brain 77 (1954 b), 1.

Penfield, W.: The twenty-ninth Maudsley lecture: The role of the temporal cortex in certain psychical phenomena. J. Ment. Sc. 101 (1955), 451.

Penfield, W.: The role of the temporal cortex in recall of past experience and interpretation of the present. Ciba Found. Sympos.: Neurological Basis of Behaviour, p. 149. Churchill, London 1958 a.

Penfield, W.: Centrencephalic integration system. Brain 81 (1958 b), 231.

Penfield, W., E. Boldrey: Somatic motor and sensory representation in the cerebral cortex of man as studied by electrical stimulation. Brain 60 (1937), 389.

BIBLIOGRAPHY

Penfield, W., T. Rasmussen: The Cerebral Cortex of Man. A Clinical Study of Localization of Function. Macmillan Co., New York 1950.

Penfield, W., L. Roberts: Speech and Brain Mechanisms. Princeton University Press 1959.

Picha, Z.: Die Begründung der psychischen Energetik. Schweiz. Zschr. Psychol. *17* (1958), 28.

Pribram, K. H., M. Bagshaw: Further analysis of temporal lobe syndrome utilizing fronto-temporal ablations. J. Comp. Neurol. *99* (1953), 347.

Pribram, K. H., K. L. Chow, J. Semmes: Limit and organization of the cortical projection from the medial thalamic nucleus in monkey. J. Comp. Neurol. *98* (1953), 433.

Rein, F. H.: Zur Physiologie des Schmerzes. Schmerz, Nark., Anaesth. *12* (1939), 129.

Roberts, W. W.: Both rewarding and punishing effects from stimulation of posterior Hypothalamus of cat with same electrode at same intensity. J. Comp. Physiol. Psychol. *51* (1958), 400.

Rose, J. E., C. N. Woolsey: The orbitofrontal cortex and its connections with mediodorsal nucleus in rabbit, sheep and cat. The frontal lobes. Res. Publ. Ass. Nerv. Ment. Dis. *27* (1948), 210.

Rose, J. E., C. N. Woolsey: Cortical connections and functional organization of the thalamic auditory system of the cat. In: Biological and Biochemical Bases of Behavior. Ed. Harlow and Woolsey, p. 127. University of Wisconsin Press 1958.

Rose, J. E., L. I. Malis, L. Kruger, Ch. P. Baker: Effects of heavy, ionizing, monoenergetic particles on the cerebral cortex. II. Histological appearance of laminar lesions and growth of nerve fibers after laminar destructions. J. Comp. Neurol. *115* (1960), 243.

Rothlin, E.: Review article. Pharmacology of lysergic acid diethylamide and some of its related compounds. J. Pharmacy Pharmacol. *9* (1957), 569.

Rothmann, H.: Zusammenfassender Bericht über den Rothmannschen grosshirnlosen Hund. Zschr. Neurol. *87* (1923), 247.

Seiferle, E.: Das Tier und die Angst. Schweiz. Arch. Tierhk. *94* (1952), 781.

Sherwood, S. L.: The relevance of some neurophysiological data to behaviour disorders. Ciba Found. Symp.: Neurological Basis of Behaviour, p. 359. Churchill, London 1958.

Smith, W. K.: The functional significance of the rostral cingular cortex as revealed by its responses to electrical excitation. J. Neurophysiol. 8 (1945), 241.

Schaltenbrand, G., S. Cobb: Clinical and anatomical studies on two cats without neocortex. Brain 53 (1930), 449.

Spindler, P.: Ausdruck und Verhalten erwachsener Zwillinge. Acta genet. med. gemell. 4 (1955), 32.

Stoll, W. A.: Beziehungen des Hypothalamus zur Temperaturregulierung. Helvet. physiol. pharmacol. acta 1 (1943), 329.

Stoll, W. A.: Lysergsäure-diäthylamid, ein Phantastikum aus der Mutterkorngruppe. Schweiz. Arch. Neurol. 60 (1947), 1.

Stoll, W. A.: Das hirnlokale Psychosyndrom im Tierexperiment. Schweiz. Ges. f. Psychiatr., 131. Vers. Genf, 1959.

Terzian, H., G. Dalle-Ore: Syndrome of Klüver and Bucy. Reproduced in man by bilateral removal of the temporal lobes. Neurology 5 (1955), 373.

Thiele, R.: Aphasie, Apraxie, Agnosie. In: Bumke, O., Hdb. d. Geisteskrankheiten 2 (1928), 243.

Tinbergen, N.: Physiologische Instinktforschung. Experientia 4 (1948), 121.

Tinbergen, N.: Instinktlehre. Vergleichende Erforschung angeborenen Verhaltens. Paul Parey, Berlin 1952.

Travis, A. M.: Neurological deficiencies following supplementary motor area lesions in Macaca mulatta. Brain 78 (1955 a), 174.

Travis, A. M.: Neurological deficiencies after ablation of the precentral motor area in Macaca mulatta. Brain 78 (1955 b), 155.

Tunturi, A. R.: Physiological determination of the arrangement of the afferent connections to the middle ectosylvian auditory area in the dog. Amer. J. Physiol. 162 (1950), 489.

Vereecken, P.: Die Störungen der Versprachlichung in der transkortikalen motorischen Aphasie. Fol. psychiat. Neerl. 61 (1958), 488.

Vogt, C. u. O.: Lebensgeschichte, Funktion und Tätigkeitsregulierung des Nucleolus. Ärztliche Forschung 1 (1947), 8 u. 43.

Walther-Büel, H.: Die Dibenaminpsychose. Mschr. Psychiatr. 118 (1949), 129.

Ward jr., A. A.: The cingular gyrus: Area 24. J. Neurophysiol. 11 (1948), 13.

Weiss, P.: Beauty and the Beast: Life and the Rule of Order. Scient. Monthly 81 (1955), 286.

Weyl, H.: Symmetry. Princeton University Press 1952.

BIBLIOGRAPHY

White, J. C.: Autonomic discharge from stimulation of the hypothalamus in man. Proc. Ass. Res. Nerv. Ment. Dis. *20* (1940), 854.

Wikler, A.: The Relation of Psychiatry to Pharmacology. Amer. Soc. Pharm. exptl. Therap. Williams & Wilkins Co., Baltimore 1957.

Woodworth, R. S., C. S. Sherrington: A pseudaffective reflex and its spinal path. J. Physiol. *31* (1904), 234.

Woolsey, C. N., E. M. Walzl: Topical projection of nerve fibers from local regions of the cochlea to the cerebral cortex of the cat. Johns Hopkins Hosp. Bull. *71* (1942), 315.

Woolsey, C. N., P. H. Settlage, D. R. Meyer, W. Sencer, T. Pinto Hamuy, A. M. Travis: Patterns of localization in precentral and "supplementary" motor areas and their relation to the concept of a premotor area. Publ. Ass. Nerv. Ment. Dis. *30* (1951), 238.

Wyss, O. A. M.: Reizphysiologische Untersuchungen an motorischer und prämotorischer Rindenzone des Affengehirns. Verhl. d. Freien Ver. schweiz. Physiologen, June 1937.

Wyss, O. A. M.: On an ipsilateral motor effect from cortical stimulation in the macaque monkey. J. Neurophysiol. *1* (1938), 125.

Wyss, O. A. M., S. Obrador: Adequate shape and rate of stimuli in electrical stimulation of the cerebral motor cortex. Amer. J. Physiol. *120* (1937), 42.

Zanchetti, A., A. Zoccolini: Autonomic hypothalamic outbursts elicited by cerebellar stimulation. J. Neurophysiol. *17* (1954), 475.

Zunini, G.: Osservazioni su di un Cane Note di Psicologia comparata. Scienze Biologiche *11*, "Vita e Pensiero," Milano 1940.

B

SUPPLEMENTARY READING

Drive-like Motives of Behavior

Brun, R.: Biologie der Angst. Schweiz. Zschr. Psychol. *4* (1945), 81.

Ebbecke, U.: Angeborene Verhaltensweisen des Menschen. Dtsch. med. Wschr. *80* (1955), 54.

Fischel, W.: Die gewaltsame Auseinandersetzung bei Hunden. Naturwissenschaftl. Rdsch. *2* (1953), 61.

Grimm, H.: Schlafstellung und Umgebungstemperatur bei der Hauskatze, Felis catus L. Zoolog. Garten (NF) *22* (1956), 171.

Haseloff, O. W.: Psychologische Gesetzmässigkeiten bei Trieb, Antrieb und Streben. Funk-Universität Rias, 1954.

Holzapfel, M.: Triebbedingte Ruhezustände als Ziel von Appetenzhandlungen. Naturwissenschaften *28* (1940), 273.

Inhelder, E.: Zur Psychologie einiger Verhaltensweisen—besonders des Spiels—von Zootieren. Zschr. Tierpsychol. *12* (1955), 88.

Klüver, H.: Behavior Mechanisms in Monkeys. University of Chicago Press 1957.

Leyhausen, P.: Verhaltensstudien an Katzen. Paul Parey Verlag, Berlin 1956.

Lorenz, K.: The comparative method in studying innate behaviour patterns. Symposia of the Soc. for Exper. Biology, *4,* Animal Behaviour, 221, 1950.

Meyer-Holzapfel, M.: Das Spiel bei Säugetieren. Kükenthal's Handbuch d. Zoologie, Bd. 8, 10. Teil, Verlagsangabe 1956.

Tinbergen, N.: An objectivistic study of the innate behaviour of animals. Bibliotheca Biotheoretica, Series D I, Part 2, 40. E. J. Brill, Leiden 1942.

Tinbergen, N.: Social Releasers and the Experimental Method required for their Study. Wilson Bull. *60* (1948), 6.

Psychic Functions and Cerebral Organization

Adrian, E. D.: The analysis of the nervous system. Proc. Roy. Soc. Med. *50* (1957), 991.

Allen, W. F.: Effect of ablating the frontal lobes, hippocampi, and occipito-parieto-temporal (excepting pyriform areas) lobes on positive and negative olfactory conditioned reflexes. Amer. J. Physiol. *128* (1940), 754.

Bard, P., M. B. Macht: The behaviour of chronically decerebrate cats. Ciba Found. Sympos.: Neurological Basis of Behaviour, p. *55.* Churchill, London 1958.

Beritoff, J.: Problems of the Modern Physiology of the Nervous and Muscle Systems. Acad. of Sciences, Georgian SSR, Tbilisi 1956.

Brodmann, K.: Vergleichende Lokalisationslehre der Grosshirnrinde. In ihren Prinzipien dargestellt auf Grund des Zellenbaues. J. A. Barth, Leipzig 1925.

Brogden, W. J., W. H. Gantt: Intraneural conditioning. Cerebellar conditioned reflexes. Arch. Neurol. Psychiatr. *48* (1942), 437.

Brun, R.: Biologie, Psychologie und Psychoanalyse. Wien. Zschr. Nervenhk. *9* (1954), 333.

Curtius, F. H. Feiereis: Zwillingsuntersuchungen über die Erbveranlagung zum vegetativ-endokrinen Syndrom der Frau (VES). Zschr. Kreislaufforschg. *49* (1960), 44.

Delgado, J. M. R.: Functional exploration of the brain with stereotaxic techniques. J. Neurosurg. *15* (1958), 269.

Eccles, J. C.: The Physiology of Nerve Cells. Johns Hopkins Press, Baltimore 1957.

Eccles, J. C.: The behaviour of nerve cells. Ciba Found. Sympos.: Neurological Basis of Behaviour. Churchill, London 1958.

Gastaut, H.: Some aspects of the neurophysiological basis of conditioned reflexes and behaviour. Ciba Found. Sympos.: Neurological Basis of Behaviour. Churchill, London 1958.

Gerard, R. W.: Physiology and psychiatry. Amer. J. Psychiatr. *106* (1949), 161.

Giljarowskij, W. A.: Die Lehre von den bedingten Reflexen und ihre Entwicklung in der russischen Psychiatrie. Psychiatr. der Gegenwart *1*, Springer, Heidelberg 1961.

Glees, P.: Morphologie und Physiologie des Nervensystems. Georg Thieme Verlag, Stuttgart 1957.

Herrick, C. J.: The Evolution of Human Nature. Austin, Univ. of Texas Press 1956.

Herrick, C. J.: Nervous mechanisms of behaviour. Fed. Proc. *20* (1961), 628.

Jung, R., O. Creutzfeldt, O. J. Grüsser: Die Mikrophysiologie kortikaler Neurone und ihre Bedeutung für die Sinnes- und Hirnfunktionen. Dtsch. med. Wschr. *82* (1957), 1050.

Karplus, J. P., A. Kreidl: Gehirn und Sympathicus. I. Mitteilung: Zwischenhirnbasis und Halssympathicus. Pflügers Arch. Physiol. *129* (1909), 139.

Lashley, K. S.: Functional determinants of cerebral localization. Arch. Neurol. Psychiatr. *38* (1937), 371.

Lashley, K. S.: Coalescence of neurology and psychology. Proc. Amer. Philosoph. Soc. *84* (1941), 461.

McCulloch, W. S.: Why the mind is in the head? L'organisation des fonctions psychiques. Publ. Marcel Monnier. Bibl. sc. Nr. 22, p. 28. Ed. du Griffon, Neuchâtel 1951.

Magoun, H. W.: Early development of ideas relating the mind with the brain. Ciba Found. Sympos.: Neurological Basis of Behaviour. Churchill, London 1958.

Malcolm, J. L.: The electrical activity of cortical neurones in relation to behaviour, as studied with microelectrodes in unrestrained cats.

Ciba Found. Sympos.: Neurological Basis of Behaviour. Churchill, London 1958.

Monnier, M.: L'organisation des fonctions psychiques à la lueur des données neurophysiologiques. Dialectica *4* (1950), Ed. du Griffon, Neuchâtel, p. 5.

Pavlov, I. P.: Conditioned reflexes. An investigation of the physiological activity of the cerebral cortex. Trans. by G. V. Anrep. Oxford University Press, London 1927.

Pavlov, I. P.: Lectures on conditioned reflexes. Trans. by W. H. Gantt. Martin Lawrence, London & International Publ. Co., New York 1928.

Pavlov, I. P.: Conditioned reflexes and psychiatry. Trans. by W. H. Gantt. International Publ. Co., New York 1941.

Sherrington, C. S.: The integrative action of the nervous system. Yale Univ. Press, New Haven 1906.

Sherrington, C. S.: Man on His Nature. Cambridge Univ. Press, 2nd ed. 1951.

Vogt, C., O. Vogt: Gestaltung der topistischen Hirnforschung und ihre Förderung durch den Hirnbau und seine Anomalien. J. Hirnforschung *1* (1954), 1.

Young, J. Z.: Die Organisation im Inneren der Nervenzellen. Endeavour *15* (1956), 5.

Synergistic Co-ordination and Competition in Collective Life

Brun, R.: Die Mechanismen der Symptombildung. A. Der Triebkonflikt. Allg. Neurosenlehre, 3. Aufl. 255, Basel 1954.

Gantt, W. H.: The Physiological Basis of Psychiatry: The Conditional Reflex. Basic Problems in Psychiatry, Edit. J. Wortis *52*, 1953.

Principles of Integral Organization in Psychic and Bodily Realms

Harlow, H. F., C. N. Woolsey: Biological and Biochemical Bases of Behavior. University of Wisconsin Press, 1958.

v. Holst, E.: Physiologie des Verhaltens. Mitteilungen aus der Max-Planck-Ges. *5* (1954), 270.

Skinner, B. F.: The Behavior of Organisms. Appleton-Century, New York 1938.

BIBLIOGRAPHY

Feeling, Sensation, and Recognition

Fischel, W.: Die Seele des Hundes. Paul Parey, Berlin und Hamburg 1950.

About Affect

Meili, R.: Angstentstehung bei Kleinkindern. Schweiz. Zschr. Psychol. *14* (1955), 195.

The Feeling and Its Functions

Bugnion, E.: Les mouvements de la face ou le mécanisme de l'expression. Georges Bridel & Co., Lausanne 1895.
Hess, W. R.: Kollektive Ordnung in biologischem Aspekt. Festschr. Max Huber, Schulthess & Co., Zürich 1944.
Jost, J.: Die James-Langesche Gefühlstheorie und ihre Auswirkungen unter besonderer Berücksichtigung der "Principles" von James. Dissert. 1951, Zürich.
Koehler, O.: Das Lächeln als angeborene Ausdrucksbewegung. Z. menschl. Vererb.- u. Konstitutionslehre *32* (1954), 390.
Leonhard, K.: Ausdruckssprache der Seele. Darstellung der Mimik, Gestik und Phonik des Menschen. Zschr. Phonetik allg. Sprachwissenschaft *5* (1951), 379.
Meyer-Holzapfel, M.: Soziale Beziehungen bei Säugetieren. Lehmann, F. E., Dalp *89*. Francke-Verlag, Bern 1958.

Memory and Intellect

Bächler, H.: Die ersten Bewohner der Schweiz. A. Francke-Verlag, Bern 1947.
Bättig, K., E. Grandjean: Der zeitliche Ablauf einer bedingten Fluchtreaktion bei der Ratte. Arch. exper. Path. Pharmak. *231* (1957), 119.
Gemelli, A.: La strutturazione del linguaggio studiata mediante l'analisi elettroacustica. Dialectica *4* (1950), 91.
Gemelli, F. A., P. S .Y. Hsiao, B. Raduscev: Contributo all'analisi dei movimenti della scrittura. Contributi del laboratorio di psicologia, Univ. Cattolica del sacro cuore *35* (1950), 109.
Hediger, H.: Dressurversuche mit Delphinen. Zschr. Tierpsychol. *9* (1952), 321.

Koehler, O.: "Zählende" Vögel und vergleichende Verhaltensforschung. Congr. Int. Orn. Basel, Acta XI, pp. 588 (1955).
Laur-Belart, R.: Bilder aus der Urgeschichte der Schweiz. Verlag Friedr. Reinhardt, Basel 1952.

Readiness To Act

Akimoto, H., O. Creutzfeldt: Reaktionen von Neuronen des optischen Cortex nach elektrischer Reizung unspezifischer Thalamuskerne. Arch. Psychiatr. *196* (1958), 494.

Bättig, K., E. Grandjean: Beziehung zwischen Alter und Erlernen einer bedingten Fluchtreaktion bei der weissen Ratte. Gerontologia *3* (1959), 266.

Beritoff, J. S.: On the origin of the central inhibition. XXI. Congr. Internac. de ciencias Fisiol., Buenos Aires 1959.

Bremer, F.: The neurophysiological problem of sleep. In: Brain Mechanisms and Consciousness, p. 137. Blackwell, Oxford 1954.

Bremer, F.: Analyse des processus corticaux de l'éveil. The Moscow Colloquium on Electroencephalography of Higher Nervous Activity, ed. H. H. Jasper, G. D. Smirnov. Supp. No. 13 Electroencephalogr. 1960.

Bremer, F., N. Stoupel, P. Ch. van Reeth: Nouvelles recherches sur la facilitation et l'inhibition des potentiels évoqués corticaux dans l'éveil réticulaire. Arch. ital. biol. *98* (1960), 229.

Christoffel, H.: Zur Psychosomatik des menschlichen Schlafs. Mschr. Psychiatr. Neurolog. *125* (1953), 329.

Collins, E. H.: Localization of an experimental hypothalamic and midbrain syndrome simulating sleep. J. Comp. Neurol. *100* (1954), 661.

Creutzfeldt, O., H. Akimoto: Konvergenz und gegenseitige Beeinflussung von Impulsen aus der Retina und den unspezifischen Thalamuskernen an einzelnen Neuronen des optischen Kortex. Arch. Psychiatr. *196* (1958), 520.

Feldberg, W.: A physiological approach to the problem of general anaesthesia and of loss of consciousness. Brit. Med. J. 1959/II, 771.

Fessard, A. E.: Mechanisms of nervous integration and conscious experience. In: Brain Mechanisms and Consciousness. Blackwell, Oxford 1954.

Gastaut, H.: The brain stem and cerebral electrogenesis in relation to consciousness. In: Brain Mechanisms and Consciousness. Blackwell, Oxford 1954.

BIBLIOGRAPHY

Jarisch, A.: Die Ohnmacht und verwandte Zustände als biologisches Problem. Klin. Med. 1948, 956.

Jasper, H.: Reticular-cortical systems and theories of the integrative action of the brain. Biological and Biochemical Bases of Behavior, ed. H. F. Harlow, C. N. Woolsey. University of Wisconsin Press 1958.

Kornmüller, A. E.: Erregbarkeitssteuernde Elemente und Systeme des Nervensystems. Grundriss ihrer Morphologie, Physiologie und Klinik. Fortschr. Neurol. *18* (1950), 437.

Magoun, H. W.: The ascending reticular system and wakefulness. In: Brain Mechanisms and Consciousness. Blackwell, Oxford 1954.

Magoun, H. W.: Non-specific brain mechanisms. In: Biological and Biochemical Bases of Behavior. University of Wisconsin Press, 1958.

Malmejac, J., P. Plane, E. Bogaert: Influence de l'anoxie et de l'ischémie sur les fonctions nerveuses supérieures. Etude expérimentale, chez le chien, à l'aide du réflexe salivaire conditionnel. Bull. Acad. Roy. Méd. Belg. *19* (1954), 11.

Moruzzi, G.: The physiological properties of the brain stem reticular system. In: Brain Mechanisms and Consciousness. Blackwell, Oxford 1954.

Nakao, H., W. P. Koella: Influence of nociceptive stimuli on evoked subcortical and cortical potentials in cat. J. Neurophysiol. *19* (1956), 187.

Parmeggiani, P. L.: Schlafverhalten bei elektrischer Reizung von Hippocampus und Corpus mammillare der nichtnarkotisierten freibeweglichen Katze. Helvet. physiol. pharmacol. acta *17* (1959), 34.

Perret, E.: Le problème psychologique et physiologique de la vigilance. Rev. Méd. Préventive *6* (1961), 23.

Rioch, D. McK.: Psychopathological and neuropathological aspects of consciousness. In: Brain Mechanisms and Consciousness. Blackwell, Oxford 1954.

Stevens, J. R., Ch. Kim, P. D. MacLean: Stimulation of caudate nucleus. Arch. Neurol. *4* (1961), 47.

Relations between Drives and Cerebral Organization

Achelis, J. D., H. v. Ditfurth: Zur "Psycho"-Physiologie des Hühnerstammhirns: Befinden und Verhalten, "Starnberger Gespräche." Thieme, Stuttgart 1961.

Alajouanine, Th.: Les grandes activités du rhinencéphale. Vol. II,

Physiologie et pathologie du rhinencéphale. Masson Cie., Paris 1961.

Anand, K., S. Dua, K. Shoenberg: Hypothalamic control of food intake (Futteraufnahme) in cats and monkeys. J. Physiol. *127* (1955), 143.

Andersson, B., P. A. Jewell, S. Larsson: An appraisal of the effects of diencephalic stimulation of conscious animals in terms of normal behaviour. Ciba Found. Sympos.: Neurological Basis of Behaviour. Churchill, London 1958.

Andersson, B., S. M. McCann: Drinking, antidiuresis and milk ejection from electrical stimulation within the hypothalamus of the goat. Acta physiol. Scand. *35* (1955), 191.

Bally, G.: Vom Ursprung und von den Grenzen der Freiheit. Eine Deutung des Spiels bei Tier und Mensch. Schwabe, Basel 1945.

Ban, T., S. Shimizu, T. Kurotsu: Experimental studies on the relationship between the Hypothalamus including area preoptica and lactation in rabbits. Med. J. Osaka Univ. *8* (1958).

Bard, Ph.: A diencephalic mechanism for the expression of rage with special reference to the sympathetic nervous system. Amer. J. Physiol. *84* (1928), 490.

Bard, Ph., V. B. Mountcastle: Some forebrain mechanisms involved in expression of rage with special reference to suppression of angry behavior. The Frontal Lobes, p. 362, ARNMD 21: Williams & Wilkins Comp., Baltimore 1948.

Blickenstorfer, E.: Mutterinstinkte bei einem Manne mit krankhafter Bildung von lactotropem Hypophysenhormon. Arch. Psychiatr. *182* (1949), 536.

Brady, J. V.: The paleocortex and behavioral motivation. Biological and Biochemical Bases of Behavior. University of Wisconsin Press 1958.

Brobeck, J. R.: Neutral factors of obesity. Bull. N.Y. Acad. Med. Ser. II, *33* (1957), 762.

Brobeck, J. R.: Regulation of feeding and drinking. Hdb. Physiol. Section I: Neurophysiology Vol. 2, 1197. Amer. Physiol. Soc., Washington 1960.

Chiray, M., Ch. Foix, J. Nicolesco: Pathologie de la région diencéphalo-mésencéphalique. Nicolesco, J.: Travaux scientifiques, 130. Masson, Paris 1959.

Delgado, J. M. R.: Emotional behavior in animals and humans. Psychiatr. Research Rep. *12* (1960), 259.

Delgado, J. M. R., W. W. Roberts, N. E. Miller: Learning motivated by electrical stimulation of the Brain. Amer. J. Physiol. *179* (1954), 3.

Dell, P.: Corrélations entre le système végétatif et le système de la vie de relation. Mesencéphale, diencéphale et cortex cérébral. J. Physiol. *44* (1952), 471.

Dell, P.: Some basic mechanisms of the translation of bodily needs into behaviour. Ciba Found. Sympos.: Neurological Basis of Behaviour. Churchill, London 1958.

Ebbecke, U.: Psychische Beeinflussung körperlicher Vorgänge. Naturwissenschaften *39* (1952), 49.

Fulton, J. F.: Frontal Lobotomy and Affective Behavior. A Neurophysiological Analysis. W. W. Norton Co., New York 1951.

Gellhorn, E.: Autonomic Regulations. Their Significance for Physiology, Psychology and Neuropsychiatry. Interscience Publ., New York 1943.

Gellhorn, E.: Prolegomena to a theory of the emotions. Perspectives Biol. Med. *4* (1961), 403.

Grastyan, E., K. Lissak, J. Szabo, G. Vereby: Über die funktionelle Bedeutung des Hippocampus. Festschrift J. Beritoff, p. 67. Publ. Acad. Sc. Georgian, SSR, Tbilisi 1956.

Harris, G. W.: Central control of pituitary secretion. Hdb. Physiol. Section I: Neurophysiology Vol. 2, 1007. Amer. Physiol. Soc., Washington 1960.

Hess, W. R., K. Akert, D. A. McDonald: Functions of the orbital gyri of cats. Brain *75* (1952), 244.

Kaada, B. R.: Somato-motor, autonomic and electrocorticographic responses to electrical stimulation of "rhinencephalic" and other structures in primates, cat and dog. A study of responses from the limbic, subcallosal, orbito-insular, piriform and temporal cortex, hippocampus-fornix and amygdala. Acta physiol. Scand. *24* (1951), Suppl. 83, 285.

Klages, W.: Frontale und diencephale Antriebsschwäche. Arch. Psychiatr. *191* (1954), 365.

Kretschmer, E.: Die Orbitalhirn- und Zwischenhirnsyndrome nach Schädelbasisfrakturen. Arch. Phychiatr. *182* (1949), 452.

Larsson, S.: On the hypothalamic organisation of the nervous mechanism regulating food intake. Acta physiol. Scand. *32* (1954), Suppl. 115, 63.

Lashley, K. S.: The thalamus and emotion. Psychol. Rev. *45* (1938), 42.

Lilly, J. C.: Learning motivated by subcortical stimulation: The start and stop patterns of behavior. Reticular formation of the brain. Internat. Sympos. Henry Ford Hosp., Detroit, Michigan, p. 705. Little Brown & Co., Boston 1958.

MacLean, P. D.: The limbic system ("visceral brain") and emotional behavior. Arch. Neurol. Psychiatr. *73* (1955), 130.

Mark, R. E.: Klinik und Therapie der vegetativen Dystonie. Springer Verlag, Wien 1954.

Martin, J. P.: Fits of laughter (sham mirth) in organic cerebral disease. Brain *73* (1950), 453.

Meyer, A. E.: Instinkt-Kollisionen im Hess'schen Reizversuch. Arch. Psychiatr. *199* (1959), 120.

Meyer-Holzapfel, M.: Die Beziehungen zwischen den Trieben junger und erwaschsener Tiere. Schweiz. Zschr. Psychol. *8* (1949), 32.

Nicolesco, J., D. Raileanu: Le système nerveux végétatif central. *Nicolesco. J.:* Travaux scientifiques, p. 278. Masson, Paris 1959.

Olds, J.: Adaptive functions of paleocortex and related structures. In: Biological and Biochemical Bases of Behavior. University of Wisconsin Press 1958.

Ploog, D.: Endogene Psychosen und Instinktverhalten. Fortschr. Neurol. *26* (1958), 83.

Soulairac, A.: Les régulations psycho-physiologiques de la faim. J. Physiol. *50* (1958), 663.

Weill, J. J. Bernfeld: Le syndrome hypothalamique. Synthèse endocrinienne métabolique, végétative et psychique. Masson & Cie., Paris 1954.

Voluntary Movements as Functional Documentation of
Cerebral Organization

Denny-Brown, D.: Motor mechanisms-Introduction: the general principles of motor integration. Handbook of Physiology. Section I: Neurophysiology, Vol. 2, p. 781. Amer. Physiol. Soc., Washington 1960.

Hess, W. R.: Die Motorik als Organisationsproblem. Biol. Zbl. *61* (1941), 545.

Jung, R., R. Hassler: The extrapyramidal motor system. Handbook of Physiology. Section I: Neurophysiology, Vol. 2, p. 863. Amer. Physiol. Soc., Washington 1960.

Lilly, J. C.: Significance of motor maps of the sensorimotor cortex in the conscious monkey. Fed. Proc. *12* (1953), 285.

Patton, H. D., V. E. Amassian: The pyramidal tract: its excitation and functions. Hdb. Physiol., Section I: Neurophysiology, Vol. 2, p. 837. Amer. Physiol. Soc., Washington 1960.

Spehlmann, R., O. D. Creutzfeldt, R. Jung: Neuronale Hemmung im motorischen Cortex nach elektrischer Reizung des Caudatum. Arch. Psychiatr. *201* (1960), 332.

Terzuolo, C. A., W. R. Adey: Sensorimotor cortical activities. Hdb. Physiol. Section I: Neurophysiology, Vol. 2, p. 797. Amer. Physiol. Soc., Washington 1960.

The Function of Sensory Systems

Adrian, E. D.: Afferent discharges to the cerebral cortex from peripheral sense organs. J. Physiol. *100* (1941), 159.

Adrian, E. D.: The Physical Background of Perception. Clarendon Press, Oxford 1947.

Beritoff, J.: Nervous Mechanisms of Spatial Orientation of Mammals. Tiflis 1959.

Bremer, F.: Les aires auditives de l'écorce cérébrale. Cours internat. d'audiol. clin. Faculté Méd. Paris. Impr. de Montligeon, La Chapelle-Montligeon 1952.

Bremer, F., V. Bonnet, C. Terzuolo: Etude électrophysiologique des aires auditives corticales du chat. Arch. internat. physiol. *62* (1954), 390.

Bremer, F., N. Stoupel: Analyse de la réponse élémentaire de l'aire visuelle du chat. J. Physiol. *48* (1956), 410.

Bremer, F., N. Stoupel: Analyse oscillographique comparée des réponses des aires de projection de l'écorce cérébrale du chat. Arch. ital. biol. *95* (1957), 3.

Burridge, W.: The ego, consciousness, and other ideals. Medicus *4* (1952), 160.

Buser, P., M. Imbert: Données sur l'organisation des projection afférentes au niveau du cortex moteur du chat. An. Fac. med. Montevideo *44* (1959), 220.

Buser, P., P. Borenstein: Réponses somesthésiques, visuelles et auditives, recueillies au niveau du cortex "associatif" suprasylvien chez le chat curarisé non anesthésié. Electroencephalogr. *11* (1959), 285.

Buser, P., P. Borenstein, J. Bruner: Étude des systèmes associatifs visuels et auditifs chez le chat anesthésié au chloralose. Electroencephalogr. *11* (1959), 305.

Clark, W. E., Le Gros: Sensory experience and brain structure. 32. Maudsley Lecture. J. Ment. Sc. *104* (1958), 13.

Creutzfeldt, O., H. Akimoto: Konvergenz und gegenseitige Beeinflussung von Impulsen aus der Retina und den unspezifischen Thalamuskernen an einzelnen Neuronen des optischen Cortex. Arch. Psychiatr. *196* (1958), 520.

Denny-Brown, D., R. A. Chambers: Visual orientation in the macaque monkey. Transactions of the Amer. Neurol. Assoc., 1959, p. 37.

Desmedt, J. E., K. Mechelse: Suppression of acoustic input by thalamic stimulation. Proc. Soc. Exper. Biol. Med. *99* (1958), 772.

Ebbecke, U.: Irradiation von Reflexen und Reflex-Empfindungen (Headsche Zonen und Hyperästhesie). Dtsch. Zschr. Nervenhk. *164* (1950), 490.

Ebbecke, U.: Vom Schmerz. Universitas *7* (1952), 159.

Gellhorn, E.: Experimentelle Untersuchungen über den Schmerz. Nervenarzt *25* (1954), 89.

Granit, R.: Receptors and Sensory Perception. Yale University Press, New Haven 1955.

Grüsser, O. J., C. Rabelo: Reaktionen retinaler Neurone nach Lichtblitzen. I. Einzelblitze und Blitzreize wechselnder Frequenz. Pflügers Arch. Physiol. *265* (1958), 501.

Grüsser, O. J., H. Kapp: Reaktionen retinaler Neurone nach Lichtblitzen. II. Doppelblitze mit wechselndem Blitzintervall. Pflügers Arch. Physiol. *266* (1958), 111.

v. Holst, E.: Aktive Leistungen der menschlichen Gesichtswahrnehmung. Studium Generale *10* (1957), 231.

Hubel, D. H., T. N. Wiesel: Integrative action in the cat's lateral geniculate body. J. Physiol. *155* (1961), 365.

Jung, R.: Mikrophysiologie des optischen Cortex: Koordination der Neuronenentladungen nach optischen, vestibulären und unspezifischen Afferenzen und ihre Bedeutung für die Sinnesphysiologie. Proc. 15. General Assembl. Jap. Med. Congr. Tokyo *5* (1959), 693.

Jung, R., G. Baumgartner: Hemmungsmechanismen und bremsende Stabilisierung an einzelnen Neuronen des optischen Cortex. Ein Beitrag zur Koordination corticaler Erregungsvorgänge. Pflügers Arch. Physiol. *261* (1955), 434.

Klüver, H.: Functional significance of the geniculostriate system. Biological Symposia *7* (1942), 253.

Krayenbühl, H., W. A. Stoll: Psychochirurgie bei unerträglichen Schmerzen. Acta neurochir. *1* (1950), 1.

BIBLIOGRAPHY

Kuffler, S. W.: Discharge patterns and functional organization of mammalian retina. J. Neurophysiol. *16* (1953), 37.

Lashley, K. S.: The mechanism of vision: XVII. Autonomy of the visual cortex. J. Genet. Psychol. *60* (1942), 197.

Lashley, K. S.: The problem of cerebral organization in vision. Biol. Symposia 7 (1942), 301.

Lindblom, U. F.: Excitability and functional organization within a peripheral tactile unit. Acta Physiol. Scand. *44* (1958), Suppl. 153, 1.

Matussek, P.: Psychopathologie II: Wahrnehmung, Halluzination und Wahn. Psychiatr. Gegenwart *1,* Springer, Heidelberg 1962.

Mountcastle, V. B., T. P. S. Powell: Central nervous Mechanisms subserving Position Sense and Kinesthesis. Bull. Johns Hopkins Hosp. *105* (1959), 173.

Pfaffmann, C.: The sense of taste. Hdb. Physiol. Section I: Neurophysiology, Vol. 1, p. 507. Amer. Physiol. Soc., Washington 1959.

Polyak, St.: The Vertebrate Visual System. University of Chicago Press 1957.

Powell, T. P. S., V. B. Mountcastle: Some aspects of the functional organization of the cortex of the postcentral gyrus of the monkey: A correlation of findings obtained in a single unit analysis with cytoarchitecture. Bull. Johns Hopkins Hosp. *105* (1959), 108.

Raman, C. V.: The perception of light and colour and the physiology of vision. Mem. Raman Res. Instit., Bangalore Nr. 125, 1960.

Ranke, O. F.: Allgemeine Physiologie der Sinnesorgane. Handbuch der gesamten Arbeitsmedizin; *1,* 207, Urban & Schwarzenberg, München 1961.

Reenpää, Y.: Theorie des Sinneswahrnehmens. Ann. Acad. Sc. Fenn. V. Med.-Anthrop. *78* (1961), 5.

Memory

Akert, K., O. S. Orth, H. F. Harlow, K. A. Schiltz: Learned behavior of rhesus monkeys following neonatal bilateral prefrontal lobotomy. Science, *132,* No. 3444 (1960), 1944.

Bättig, K., E. Grandjean: Der zeitliche Ablauf einer bedingten Fluchtreaktion bei der Ratte. Arch. exper. Path. Pharmak. *231* (1957), 119.

Benjamin, R. M.: Absence of deficits in taste discrimination following cortical lesions as a function of the amount of preoperative practice. J. Comp. Physiol. Psychol. (in Press).

Benjamin, R. M., R. F. Thompson: Effects of cortical lesions in infant and adult cats on roughness discrimination. Amer. Physiologist *1* (1958), 80.

Bremer, F., J. Brihaye, G. André-Balisaux: Physiologie et pathologie du corps calleux. Schweiz. Arch. Neurol. *78* (1956), 31.

Eccles, J. C.: The physiology of imagination. Scient. American *199* (1958), 135.

Jasper, H. H., G. F. Ricci, B. Doane: Patterns of cortical neuronal discharge during conditioned responses in monkeys. Ciba Found. Sympos. Neurological Basis of Behaviour. Churchill, London 1958.

Lashley, K. S.: In search of the engram. Symposia of the Soc. for Exper. Biology *4,* Animal Behaviour (1950), 454.

Pribram, K. H.: The intrinsic systems of the forebrain. Hdb. Physiol. Section I: Neurophysiology, Vol. 2, p. 1323. Amer. Physiol. Soc., Washington 1960.

Russell, W. R.: The physiology of memory. Proc. Royal Soc. Med. *51* (1957), 9.

Tönnies, J. F.: Die Erregungssteuerung im Zentralnervensystem. Erregungsfokus der Synapse und Rückmeldung als Funktionsprinzipien. Arch. Psychiatr. *182* (1949), 478.

Senso-Memo-Motoric: Intelligent Behavior and Language

Akert, K., E. M. Mortimer: Zentrale Einwirkungen auf die Muskeltätigkeit. Bull. Schweiz. Akad. Med. Wiss. *16* (1960), 337.

Akert, K., R. A. Gruesen, C. N. Woolsey, D. R. Meyer: Klüver-Bucy syndrome in monkeys with neocortical ablations of temporal lobe. Brain *84,* Part III (1961), 480.

Beritoff, J.: Problems of the modern physiology of the nervous and muscle systems. Publ. Acad. Sc. Georgian SSR Tbilisi 1956.

Bremer, F.: De la sensation à l'action. Bull. Acad. roy. Belg. *45* (1959), 1148.

Conrad, K.: Das Problem der gestörten Wortfindung in Gestalt theoretischer Betrachtung. Schweiz. Arch. Psychiatr. *63* (1949), 141.

Derwort, A.: Aphasie, Agnosie und Aparaxie. Psychiatr. Gegenwart, *1,* Springer, Heidelberg 1962.

Halstead, W. C.: Brain and Intelligence: A Quantitative Study of the Frontal Lobes. University of Chicago Press, Chicago 1947.

BIBLIOGRAPHY

v. Holst, E., H. Mittelstaedt: Das Reafferenzprinzip. (Wechselwirkungen zwischen Zentralnervensystem und Peripherie). Naturwissenschaften *37* (1950), 464.

Kayser, Ch.: Langage parlé. Manuel de Physiologie. Édit. Flammarion, Paris (in press).

Koehler, O.: Vom Erbgut der Sprache. HOMO *5* (1954), 97.

Koehler, O.: Vorbedingungen und Vorstufen unserer Sprache bei Tieren. Verh. Deutsch, Zoolog. Ges. Tübingen (1954), 327.

Lashley, K. S.: Dynamic processes in perception. In: Brain Mechanisms and Consciousness, p. 422. Blackwell, Oxford 1954.

Luria, A. R.: Verbal regulation of behavior. In: The central nervous system and behavior. Transact. 3rd Conference, New York, Ed. M. A. B. Breja, Josiah Macy, Jr., 1960.

Minkowski, M.: L'élaboration du système nerveux. In: Les étapes du développement psychique. Vol. 8, Encyclopédie française. Sect. A: Organization somato-psychique, Paris 1938.

Wagner, R.: Probleme und Beispiele biologischer Regelung. G. Thieme, Stuttgart 1954.

Cerebral Organization and Integral Individuality

Bättig, K.: Die Anbahnung einer bedingten Fluchtreaktion bei der Ratte. Helvet. physiol. pharmacol. acta *15* (1957), 251.

Beringer, K.: Der Meskalinrausch—seine Geschichte und Erscheinungsweise. Springer, Berlin 1927.

Bleuler, M.: Die Ähnlichkeit zwischen den endokrien und hirnlokalen Psychosyndromen und ihre theoretische Bedeutung. Folia Psychiatr. Neerl. *56* (1953), 593.

Bleuler, M.: Endokrinologische Psychiatrie. Psychiatr. Gegenwart *1*, Springer, Heidelberg 1962.

de Boor, W.: Pharmakopsychologie und Psychopathologie. Springer, Berlin 1956.

Bovet, D.: Relations d'isostérie et Phénomènes compétitifs dans le domaine des médicaments du système nerveux végétatif et dans celui de la transmission neuromusculaire. Les Prix Nobel 1957, Stockholm 1958.

Curtius, F., K. H. Krüger: Das vegetativ-endokrine Syndrom der Frau. Urban & Schwarzenberg, München 1952.

Eccles, J. C.: The Neurophysiological Basis of Mind: The Principles of Neurophysiology. Clarendon Press, Oxford 1953.

Eccles, J. C.: The physiology of imagination. Scientific American *199* (1958), 135.

Fleisch, A. O.: Die Persönlichkeit Akromegaloider. Schweiz. med. Wschr. *82* (1952), 230.

Harris, G. W., R. P. Michael, Patricia P. Scott: Neurological site of action of stilbestrol in eliciting sexual behaviour. Ciba Found. Sympos.: Neurological Basis of Behaviour, p. 236. Churchill, London 1958.

Hauser, E. H.: Zur Kenntnis der psychischen Wirkung von Sexualhormonen in hohen Dosen. Inaug.-Diss. Zürich 1951.

Hunt, H. F.: Physiology and drug action: behavioral implications. Fed. Proc. *19* (1960), 2.

Lopez-Ibor, J. J.: Psychosomatische Forschung. Psychiatr. Gegenwart *1,* Springer, Heidelberg 1962.

Minz, B.: Le rôle de l'élément adrénergique dans la physiologie et la physiopathologie du système nerveux central. Biol. Méd. *48* (1959), 577.

Møller, K. O.: Rauschgifte und Genussmittel. Benno Schwabe, Basel 1951.

Ploog, D.: Verhaltensforschung und Psychiatrie. Psychiatr. Gegenwart *1,* Springer, Heidelberg 1962.

Rosenzweig, M. R., D. Krech, E. L. Bennett: Brain enzymes and adaptive behaviour. Ciba Found. Sympos.: Neurological Basis of Behaviour, Churchill, London 1958.

Psychodynamic Principles

Brazier, M. A. B.: A neuronal basis for ideas. Bibl. Sc. *22,* Griffon, Neuchâtel 1951.

Durig, A.: Vom Chaos zum Menschen. 1. Österreich. Ärztetagung, Sept. 1947, Salzburg.

Gantt, W. H.: Principles of physiological learning. Abstracts of Communications, XIX Intern. Physiol. Congr. Montreal 1953.

Herrick, C. J.: Mechanisms of nervous adjustment. Bibl. Sc. *22,* Griffon, Neuchâtel 1951.

Hess, W. R.: Die physiologische Grundlage der Psychosomatik. Dtsch. med. Wschr. *86* (1961), 3.

Kretschmer, E.: Kausale und phänomenologische Begriffsbildung in der Hirnphysiologie. Nervenarzt *22* (1951), 9.

Leyhausen, P.: Die Entdeckung der relativen Koordination: Ein Beitrag

BIBLIOGRAPHY

zur Annäherung von Physiologie und Psychologie. Studium Generale 7 (1954), 45.

Lorenz, K.: Über die Entstehung auslösender "Zeremonien." Die Vogelwarte *1* (1951), 9.

McCulloch, W. S.: Why the mind is in the head? Bibl. Sc. *22*, Griffon, Neuchâtel 1951.

Magoun, H. W.: Early development of ideas relating the mind with the brain. Neurological Basis of Behaviour. Churchill, London 1958.

Monnier, M.: L'organisation des fonctions psychiques à la lueur des données neurophysiologiques. Bibl. Sc. *22*, Griffon, Neuchâtel 1951.

Wilde, K.: Psychologische Gesetzmässigkeiten bei Trieb, Antrieb und Streben. Rias, 1954.

Ordering Forces

Eccles, J. C.: Hypotheses relating to the brain-mind problem. Nature *168* (1951), 53.

Keidl, W. D.: Grenzen der Übertragbarkeit der Regelungslechre auf biologische Probleme. Naturwissenschaften *48* (1961), 264.

Mittelstaedt, H.: Die Regelungstheorie als methodisches Werkzeug der Verhaltensanalyse. Naturwissenschaften *48* (1961), 246.

Stegemann, J.: Die Regelung der retinalen Beleuchtungsstärke. Naturwissenschaften *48* (1961), 254.

Wiener, N.: Über Informationstheorie. Naturwissenschaften *48* (1961), 174.

Kybernetik *1*, H. 1, Springer, Berlin 1961.

Mechanisation of Thought Processes I + II. Symposium 10, of Nat. Physical Lab. Her Majesty's Stationery Office, London 1959.

C

GENERAL WORKS IN CHRONOLOGICAL ORDER

Zeitschrift für Tierpsychologie. Paul Parey, Berlin.

Bleuler, E.: Naturgeschichte der Seele und ihres Bewusstwerdens, 2nd ed. Springer, Berlin 1932.

Morgan, C. T.: Physiological Psychology. McGraw-Hill Book Co., New York 1943.

v. Wyss, W. H.: Psychophysiologische Probleme in der Medizin. Schwabe, Basel 1944.

Roger, H.: Eléments de Psycho-Physiologie. Masson et Cie., Paris 1946.

Gemelli, A., G. Zunini: Introduzione alla psicologia. "Vita e Pensiero," Milano 1947.

Freeman, G. L.: Physiological Psychology. D. van Nostrand Co., New York 1948.

Gantt, W. H.: Physiological psychology. Ann. Rev. Physiol. *10* (1948), 453.

McDowall, R. J. S.: Sane Psychology: A Biological Introduction to Psychology. John Murray, London 1948.

Hebb, D. O.: The Organization of Behavior: A Neuropsychological Theory. John Wiley, Sons, New York 1949.

Lorenz, K. Z: Ganzheit und Teil in der tierischen und menschlichen Gemeinschaft. Studium Generale *3* (1950), 31.

Katz, D.: Handbuch der Psychologie. Schwabe, Basel 1951.

Cerebral Mechanisms in Behavior. The Hixon Symposium. Chapman & Hall, London; John Wiley & Sons, New York 1951.

Bykow, K. M.: Grosshirnrinde und innere Organe. VEB Verlag Volk u. Gesundheit, Berlin 1952.

Ceni, C.: Evoluzione Biologica della Psiche. Licinio Capelli, Bologna 1952.

Eccles, J. C.: The Neurophysiological Basis of Mind. The Principles of Neurophysiology, Oxford University Press, London 1953.

Gellhorn, E.: Factors modifying conditioned reactions and their relation to the autonomic nervous system. Ann. N. Y. Acad. Sc. *56* (1953), 200.

Rohracher, H.: Die Arbeitsweise des Gehirns und die psychischen Vorgänge. J. A. Barth, München 1953.

Jung, R.: Allgemeine Neurophysiologie: Die Tätigkeit des Nervensystems. Hdb. Inn. Med. Vol. V/1, 4th ed. Springer, Berlin 1953.

Herrick, C. J.: Psychology from a biologist's point of view. Psychol. Rev. *62* (1955), 5.

v. Wyss, W. H.: Aufgaben und Grenzen der psychosomatischen Medizin. Springer, Berlin 1955.

Klüver, H.: Behavior Mechanisms in Monkeys. University of Chicago Press, 1933, 1957.

Schneirla, T. C.: The Concept of Development in Comparative Psychology: An Issue in the Study of Human Behavior. University of Minnesota Press, Minneapolis 1957.

Hebb, D. O.: A Textbook of Psychology. W. B. Saunders Co., Philadelphia 1958.

Gestaltungen sozialen Lebens bei Tier und Mensch. Francke, Bern 1958.

Schneirla, T. C.: The Study of Animal Behavior: Its History and Relation to the Museum. I & II. Curator 4, 1958 and II/1, 1959.

Legait, H.: Contribution à l'étude morphologique et expérimentale du système hypothalomo-neurohypophysaire de la poule Rhode-Island. Thèse, Univ. Catholique de Louvain 1959.

Rothschuh, K. E.: Theorie des Organismus: Bios, Psyche, Pathos. Urban & Schwarzenberg, München 1959.

Wieser, W.: Organismen, Strukturen, Maschinen. Fischer-Bücherei 230, 1959.

Arnold, M. B.: Emotion and Personality. Vol. I: Psychological Aspects. Vol. II: Neurological and Physiological Aspects. Columbia University Press, New York 1960.

INDEX